MONEY AS
EMOTIONAL CURRENCY

Money as Emotional Currency is one of a series of low-cost books under the title PSYCHOANALYTIC **ideas** that brings together the best of public lectures and other writings given by analysts of the British Psycho-Analytical Society on important psychoanalytic subjects.

MONEY AS EMOTIONAL CURRENCY

Edited by

Anca Carrington

KARNAC

First published in 2015 by
Karnac Books Ltd
118 Finchley Road, London NW3 5HT

British Library Cataloguing in Publication Data

A C.I.P. for this book is available from the British Library

ISBN 978 1 78220 200 4

Edited, designed and produced by The Studio Publishing Services Ltd
www.publishingservicesuk.co.uk
e-mail: studio@publishingservicesuk.co.uk

Printed in Great Britain

www.karnacbooks.com

CONTENTS

ACKNOWLEDGEMENTS

I am grateful to James Rose for his constant and gentle support, and for his sustained trust in this work.

I would like to thank the *International Journal of Psychoanalysis* for permission to reproduce the paper by David Tuckett and Richard Taffler, "Phantastic objects and the financial market's sense of reality: a psychoanalytic contribution to the understanding of stock market instability"; Penguin for permission to reproduce Jorge Luis Borges's short story "The Zahir", from *The Aleph* (London: Penguin Books, 2000); *Free Associations* for permission to reproduce Gilles Arnaud's paper "Money as signifier: A Lacanian insight into the monetary order".

To Simon

Giles Arnaud is a professor at ESCP (Ecole Superieure de Commerce) in Paris, and specialises in the application of Lacanian psychoanalytic theory to organisations, work and professional life.

Jorge Luis Borges (1899–1986) was an Argentine writer internationally recognised for his short stories, essays and poetry.

Anca Carrington is a psychotherapist who trained at the Tavistock Centre in London, after a career as an economist, both in academia and the civil service.

Sigmund Freud (1856–1939) was an Austrian neurologist who gained international recognition as the founding father of psychoanalysis.

James Rose is a psychoanalyst, Fellow of the Institute of Psycho-analysis in London. Before becoming a psychoanalyst, he was involved in organisational research and consultancy in a local government context. He is editor of the Psychoanalytic Ideas series published by Karnac.

Richard Taffler is a professor at Warwick Business School and specialises in behavioural and emotional finance, where he emphasises the role of the unconscious in investment decisions and market behaviour.

David Tuckett is a psychoanalyst, Fellow of the Institute of Psychoanalysis in London, Professor and Director of the Centre for the Study of Decision-Making Uncertainty at UCL.

PREFACE

The importance of money and our relationship to it have become impossible to ignore in a decade defined by global economic crisis and financial instability.

Integrating a psychoanalytic perspective with insights offered by economics, this book aims to contribute to a debate towards a better understanding of money in its dual functioning: as omnipresent component of our external reality, as well as powerful agent of our emotional responses.

The main argument proposed is that the intense and complex emotional charge that money can engender stems from the role that money has, not so much in the external world, but in a primarily internal economy ruled by unconscious fantasy, where every external transaction has an internal, emotional counterpart, whose impact is mysterious, deep, and far reaching.

The book explores the trace of the emotional undercurrent stirred by money from its beginnings in childhood to its consolidation into adult life, through love and work, for individuals and society alike, and with an emphasis on ordinary development, rather than on pathology. Bringing together Freud's seminal work with more recent applications of psychoanalytic thinking to financial markets, with

Borges' prose and Lacanian insights, this book crosses boundaries of discipline and schools of thought in order to allow new connections to emerge and fresh understandings to develop.

Introduction

Anca Carrington

Before linking it to its monetary connotation, the *Oxford English Dictionary* defines "currency" as a noun denoting the fact or condition of flowing. This dynamic quality, this restlessness and identity of motion, is also in the nature of money and constitutes an important reason for which the subject matter has escaped conventional scrutiny for so long. The current is fast and strong, and by the time we observe it in its outward manifestations, it has already travelled far and deep, carrying with it rich traces of a distant mystery.

It is, thus, that, while an undisputed component of reality, be it shared or individual, money is something we cannot fail to recognise, yet we remain unable to fully define or comprehend. Concrete and functional definitions abound, but these leave out an important consideration, which is that beyond its more accessible, pragmatic configuration, money is primarily an emotional entity. In this domain, its register is a wide one, from good to bad, from powerful to restricting, hopeful to depressing, exhilarating and sexy to frightening. Indeed, it is the force of these very emotions, that congregate around money like stubborn moths around a late light on a summer's night, that might explain our difficulty with really thinking about and understanding money, allowing it, instead, to remain society's last taboo (Krueger, 1991), "as mysterious as sex, as steeped in ritual as religion and as volatile as politics" (Yablonsky, 1991, p. 66). Krueger describes money as "probably the most emotionally meaningful object in contemporary life . . . imbued by each individual with a number of unconscious equations" (Krueger, 1996, p. 3), which manifest in its "personal multi-determined meanings" (Krueger, 1991, p. 209).

The power of the forbidding force of money as emotional currency is well measured by the fact that psychoanalysts themselves, defined by daring to think about what most others shy away from, have been cautious about applying their trade to this aspect of reality, and only wrote about it sparsely and in prescribed ways, either around the issue of fees, or along the lines of pathology linked to explicit troubles patients present in relating to money: miserliness, overspending, inordinate generosity, bargain hunting, gambling.

So, what is it that makes it so difficult to think and talk about money, other than in technical terms? I propose that the barriers to thinking and talking about money with any degree of ease are built out of a mixture of deep and potent fear, shame and disgust, common to us all, not just to those who become analytic patients, and by no means bypassing analysts or psychotherapists. Some of the fear is in the nature of encountering something akin to a deep, inaccessible, raw force. Indeed, Brodsky (1986) identifies money as a quintessential ingredient of reality, as inescapable as the forces of nature: "Along with air, earth, water and fire, money is the fifth natural force a human being has to reckon with most often" (p. 157, cited in Žižek, 2009, pp. 80–81). Shame stems from the naked proximity to such a force, as creative and forbidden as the primal scene, as well as from the greed and the sense of exposure that the excitement it generates engenders. As for disgust, it is the linking of money to faeces that, while making Freud known to most, both offers an explanation and shuts an avenue of thought almost simultaneously.

Integrating a psychoanalytic perspective with insights offered by economics, this book aims to contribute to a debate that can help us develop a better understanding of money as internal and external object. The main argument put forward here is that the sense of greed, fear, shame, and disgust that is so common when the topic of money is near, stems from the role that money has not so much in the external world, but in an internal economy ruled by phantasy and whose foundations are as old as the beginning of the psyche itself.

A secondary aim of this book is to allow the prevailing (mostly Kleinian) and the Lacanian perspectives to come together in ways that can further our understanding of the world and our being in it, thus gaining more than any single perspective can deliver. This is a deliberate choice, and a move away from partisan writing that is often caught in the taxing tension of dissent and controversy that tends to accompany the interaction between alternative approaches to analytic work (Bernardi, 2002).

When referring to this apparent divide between an internal world and an external one, I have in mind both the Kleinian view of the body as a recipient or container and the Lacanian view of this perceived binary opposition as a Moebius strip, a continuum where the inside and outside can never be separated. In either case, money is most apt at navigating the topography of our emotional experience, through the vehicle of phantasy, understood as an imaginary scene where the subject is the protagonist and which offers the fulfilment of a wish (Laplanche & Pontalis, 1988, p. 314). When this wish is conscious, we speak of daydreams. However, more often than not, these wishes belong to the unconscious realm, and are commonly designated in the literature as *phantasy*, in an attempt to distinguish them from conscious processes. Freud (1908e) specifies the aim of phantasy as wish-fulfilment: "The motive forces of phantasies are unsatisfied wishes and every single phantasy is the fulfilment of a wish, a correction of unsatisfying reality" (p. 146). He links this to the role of play in childhood, which stands in clear relationship to reality through an anchoring process which links "imagined objects and situations to the tangible and visible things of the real world" (p. 144). As this book aims to illustrate, money is the anchor of choice for a very important set of universal phantasies.

In the current literature, the meaning of this concept is by no means unanimously agreed upon. Here, I use the term *phantasy* in its wide sense, encompassing both Freud's understanding of it as imagined gratification of frustrated desires, as well the more recent view, which incorporates representations of unorganised primitive experience (Hayman, 1989). An important addition from Lacan in this respect is the recognition of meaning carried by phantasy, which is ultimately "an image set to work in a signifying structure" ("*image mise en function dans la structure signifiante*", Lacan, 1966a, p. 114): that is, an entity that takes its meaning from its relative position in our mental structure.

In other words, money functions as a gateway between two worlds, an internal one dominated by mostly unresolved, unruly, and deep conflicts, and an external one, where the semblance of some degree of control is possible, albeit very difficult to sustain. It is not the outward meaning of money that we are uncomfortable with, but the deeper one—the dark side of the coin.

External transactions in the economic domain remain, throughout life, linked to these deeper and more fundamental internal exchanges, with money an apt and much needed vehicle on both levels, as the one external object that can instantly take on the role of currency for as many internal transactions as it does externally. Indeed, it could be argued that its main attraction is not in its ability to facilitate rational, conscious, economic transactions, but most of all in its power to moderate unconscious ones, whether libidinal or destructive. As Buchan (1997) aptly sums this up, money is used in peacetime to build, and in wartime to destroy (p. 249).

What makes money such a powerful emotional entity is its ability to attend to both sets of drives, and to operate as a vehicle for desire, as well as an instrument of aggression, both of which are almost universally subject to an armoury of defences. Indeed, it could be argued that, ordinarily, money acts as a socially acceptable defence against the pressures that both desire and hostility create in us as individuals and as a society.

Located on the boundary between the concrete and the symbolic domains, money provides the means for managing our many anxieties, originating in the earliest stages of our living experience, and daily encountered and negotiated throughout life. Indeed, anxiety itself has the attributes of money, as it functions as "the universal currency of affect, in the sense that every emotion can be converted into it" (Fink, 1997, p. 215).

Thus, our relationship to money carries an expression of our deepest connection to a sense of internal plenty or deprivation, of our most basic experience of being able to access and sustain life-giving supplies, or of failing ever to reach a sense of securely being provided for. But most of all, money has the desirable attributes of a navigation system of recurrent oedipal configurations and their intrinsic anxieties, as it allows us to negotiate their triangular challenges in a way that either denies the idea of the third, or bypasses the fear of losing one's potency, the pain of not being the chosen one, or channels the violence that simmers underneath every encounter that frustrates the pleasure principle.

When I refer to the oedipal configuration, I have in mind both the classical view of the Oedipus complex as an "organised body of loving and hostile wishes which the child experiences towards its parents" (Laplanche & Pontalis, 1988, p. 282), structured around desire for one parent and rivalry with the other, as well as the Lacanian one, which regards this as "the paradigmatic triangular structure, which contrasts with all dual relationships" (Evans, 1996, p. 127).

Segal (1989) identifies this complex as the centre of psychoanalytic work, in a way that mirrors the central place that money has in economic life. The way she links the experience of the Oedipus complex to the loving and destructing drives of early life, much explored by Melanie Klein, mirrors the way in which an equally often-cited economist described money: "Money is a singular thing. It ranks with love as man's greatest sources of joy and with death as his greatest source of anxiety" (Galbraith, 1979, p. 161). Both the Oedipus myth and our daily relationship to money are characterised by blindness to the driving forces involved, by a fundamental avoidance of knowledge where uncomfortable truths are concerned. In other words, they share what Lacan has labelled a "passion for ignorance" (Felman, 1987).

In Freud (1924d), we learn that, in ideal circumstances, the Oedipus complex dissolves in a way which amounts to "a destruction and an abolition of the complex", but that "If the ego has in fact not achieved much more than a *repression* of the complex, the latter persists in an unconscious state in the id and will later manifest its pathogenic effect" (p. 399).

Unlike Freud, I do not believe that the Oedipus complex can ever be abolished or that its resurfacing is purely a matter of pathology. Instead, I propose that, if all goes well in early development, the complex becomes attenuated—perhaps Freud's less satisfactory solution of repression is the only possible one—only to resurface in ordinary life, and not exclusively in pathology and in the consulting room, each time the emotional geometry fits its (triangular) structure.

Specifically, money can act as both defence and fantasy/phantasy vehicle, attending to both our aggressive and vulnerable states. Wiseman (1974) identifies four main such fantasies (which he calls dreams) facilitated by money: (i) "achieving endless security, where money embodies the promise of a glorious self-sufficiency" (p. 18), akin to the generous state of plenty that precedes the move from the binary infant–mother relationship to a triangular structure defined by loss; (ii) "showing them all" (p. 18), where riches become a defence against the humiliation of not being all that mother desires; (iii) making oneself lovable, where money, as the transformation agent, has the power to turn us into the desired ones; (v) revenge and becoming the greatest/biggest, where money can impose limits on others and give a socially acceptable manifestation to the wish to destroy or annihilate the opponent, as embodiment of the object of mother's desire (think mergers and acquisitions in the world of business). The fulfilment of each of these dreams is tantamount to the dreamer never being troubled by the challenges of a third presence, never having to fight to retain a plentiful supply of love and strength.

Perhaps the easiest way to see the link between money and desire is through Lacan's concept of *objet petit a*, the object cause of desire on to which a multitude of ideas and fantasies may be pinned. In this sense, money is the ideal candidate, as, on this level, it is not the intrinsic object—the metal, the paper, the plastic, or electronic impulse—that is of interest, but its desirable qualities. In Lacan's (1959) words, "The object of desire in the usual sense is either a fantasy which supports the desire, or a lure" (cited in Bailly, 2009, p. 129), like Plato's *agalma*, the valuable offering made to the Greek gods, in a container of no intrinsic value (Bailly, 2009, p. 131). Lacan (2013) defines the agalma as "the object the subject believes his desire aims at and regarding which he most completely mistakes the object for the cause of desire" (p. 70).

In Buchan's (1997) poetic words,

> a banknote may describe to one person a drink in a pub, a fairground ride to another, to a third a diamond ring, an act of charity to a fourth, relief from prosecution to a fifth and, to a sixth, simply the sensation of comfort and security. (p. 18)

We find it easy to understand and accept this, as if things could never be another way, and it remains a mystery what the first coins were for, or how money emerged as "the champion means of communicating needs and wishes" (p. 28), as its origin is in myth rather than history.

The discussion opens in Chapter One with an overview of the functions that money plays in the external economy and their possible emotional counterparts. Externally, money that is easily flowing and plentiful constitutes a sign of a developed, healthy economy. Likewise, internally, it can create, or at least promise, a sense of safety and resourcefulness. Economic crisis and financial instability threaten our external and internal realities alike, whether we experience these collectively or individually. It is by exploring the fear of losing money as much as the wish of gaining it that we develop some true under-standing of this most elusive entity. While its functions in the external, real economy have long been identified and defined, the role money plays in our internal reality has remained less explored, although both its presence and its absence shape and alter not only our external circumstances, but also our internal emotional landscape. It is the emotional meaning of money and its role as currency in the internal economy that the first chapter focuses on.

This is followed by a return to Freud's key contributions to the psychoanalytic thinking on money matters in Chapter Two, which includes the 1908 paper on "Character and anal erotism" and the 1917 one, "On transformations of instinct as exemplified in anal erotism". As we are reminded in the introduction to the *Standard Edition* of the first of these two contributions, it is easy to forget the astonishment and indignation with which Freud's ideas were received at the time. Something of the kind might be still evoked in today's readers, however accustomed they might be to the often simplified and publi-cised link between money and faeces attributed to Freud. Yet, it is these very contributions, however intriguing they might seem at first sight, that enable us to establish a relationship between the way in which we relate to money as adults, and the childhood experience of encountering the world through the language of the body. Freud's second paper adds to and elaborates the first, illustrating his charac-teristic way of developing his thinking over time by refining and revisiting old themes, never satisfied that he has reached the ultimate explanation. The fluidity with which he shows the unconscious mind to equate faeces with money, babies, and the penis provides the link from the dual mother–baby relationship—where absence and pres-ence are the key anxieties—to the triangular configuration of the Oedipus complex, where one's own desire and place in the other's desire are defining, with the third now identified as the reason for the changes in the experience we have of our first interaction with another being. As the graph in this second paper depicts, the move towards money is one of development along the axis of object relating.

Chapter Three brings to life Freud's theoretical formulations, by providing an overview of a vivid illustration of the endless activity of the phantasy domain in childhood and its seamless and intricate weaving of internal and external realities, shaped by the triangular geometry of desire. The chapter takes its main inspiration from the concluding chapter of a book, *Phantasy in Childhood* (Davidson & Fay, 1952), titled "The living through of phantasies". Through a discussion of the predominant phantasy themes that can be identified in the carefully observed development of an ordinary little girl that Davidson and Fay provide, Rose and Carrington offer fresh insight into the ways in which interpersonal transactions are negotiated from the beginning of life, starting with the mother–baby dyad, through the Oedipal configurations of her relating to both parents, and, later on, through the challenges brought by sibling rivalry. This is a reflection on the story of ordinary development, which makes it a very poignant account of the pervasiveness of the emerging structures of phantasy in the universal unconscious experience.

Chapter Four follows the shaping of such phantasies in adult life, and tracks their impact on our shared experience of economic life. The seminal paper by Tuckett and Taffler (2008) reproduced here explores the cross-over between the external and internal economies in the form of phantastic objects that, while originating in early psychic life, have come to dominate the financial markets and, indirectly, all our lives over the past decade. Central to their argument is the role of narratives in organising human experience, with unconscious phantasy as their template rooted in childhood. Using psychoanalytic understanding of how reality is experienced in different states of mind, the authors analyse the role of attitudes of mind and emotional responses to shaping outcomes in the financial markets.

This is followed by an intimate account of the relationship between love, money, and identity in a short story by Borges (1949), in Chapter Five. "The Zahir"—a currency of many meanings and of fluid desire that escapes satisfaction—is the epitome of a symbol that challenges the order of time and space, returning again and again at the unsettling gateway between phantasy and reality, between the internal and external worlds. The mysterious coin arises at a place of contrast, where the juxtaposition of incompatible elements has the quality of dream and unconscious construction. At the same time, the story itself, with its "as if" quality, and the emphasised gravity and authority of the narrator's voice, urges the reader to believe in it for it to work its magic, just as money needs our trust and belief in order to maintain and fulfil its role. The woman whose loss the money distracts from has herself something of the quality of money, her success followed by her being taken out of circulation, made obsolete by time and change. Yet, what money replaces time and again is more of the same, without escape, and underneath it all is a familiar story, that of a man who killed his own father, who had, in turn, "used his magic to usurp an infinite treasure to himself" (p. 83). We are left wondering which story is the truth: the story that contains the other, or the story within. A possible answer is in the inscription on the coin, the two that eliminates the third.

In a return to Freud, the final chapter, Chapter Six, contributes a Lacanian take on money in relationship to desire and the lack. A brief introduction to key elements of this analytic approach is followed by a detailed contribution by Gilles Arnaud, previously published in 2003. In this, he invites us to move beyond the limitations and constraints of the overly exclusive view that links money to anality. He distinguishes between money as a sign of merchandise and exchange, of wealth and value, and its role as currency of desire and vehicle of its endless fluidity. In the latter domain, we are shown how money can function as a defence, facilitating the denial of loss and preserving a phantasy of omnipotence. Arnaud discusses Lacan's (1966b) famous seminar on the purloined letter, based on Poe's story, which identifies money as the one object whose very possession is inscribed with loss. The link to the unconscious is explored in his analysis of the similarity between money and language, which, according to Lacan, is the structure by which the unconscious itself is defined, whereby each entity takes its meaning from its relative place in the totality of entities.

Whether understood in the generic or Lacanian sense, the fundamental quality of the symbolic domain to our very being relates not so much to it acting as territory in which we can communicate with others, but to the access it offers to a system whereby we can make sense of our very own place in the world and, thus, tackle a most fundamental source of uncertainty. It is here, on the boundary between the internal and external worlds of our everyday life, that money weaves its magic and casts its spell, something we need to allow in order to remain anchored to the network of symbols and meaning that social life creates, but also something that we can try to understand, without losing our sense of place, order, and meaning.

References

Arnaud, G. (2003). Money as signifier: A Lacanian insight into the monetary order. *Free Associations*, 10(1): 25–44.

Bailly, L. (2009). *Lacan: A Beginner's Guide*. Oxford: Oneworld.

Bernardi, R. (2002). The need for true controversies in psychoanalysis: the debates on Melanie Klein and Jacques Lacan in the Río de la Plata. *International Journal of Psychoanalysis*, 83: 851–873.

Borges, J. L. (1949). The Zahir. In: Borges, J. L. (2000), *The Aleph*. London: Penguin.

Brodsky, J. (1986). *Less than One: Selected Essays*. New York: Farrar Straus and Giroux.

Buchan, J. (1997). *Frozen Desire: An Inquiry into the Meaning of Money*, London: Picador.

Davidson, A., & Fay, J. (1952). *Phantasy in Childhood*. Westport, CT: Greenwood Press (1972).

Evans, D. (1996). *An Introductory Dictionary of Lacanian Psychoanalysis*. London: Routledge.

Felman, S. (1987). *Jacques Lacan and the Adventure of Insight: Psychoanalysis in Contemporary Culture*. Cambridge, MA: Harvard University Press.

Fink, B. (1997). *A Clinical Introduction to Lacanian Psychoanalysis: Theory and Technique*. London: Harvard University Press.

Freud, S. (1908b). Character and anal erotism. *S.E.*, 9: 169–175. London: Hogarth.

Freud, S. (1908e). Creative writers and day-dreaming. *S.E.*, 9: 143–153. London: Hogarth.

Freud, S. (1917c). On transformations of instinct as exemplified in anal erotism. *S.E.*, 17: 125–134. London: Hogarth.

Freud, S. (1924d). The dissolution of the Oedipus complex. *S.E.*, 13: 173–182. London: Hogarth.

Galbraith, J. K. (1979). *The Age of Uncertainty*. Boston, MA: Houghton Miffin.

Hayman, A. (1989). What do we mean by 'phantasy'? *International Journal of Psychoanalysis*, 70: 105–114.

Krueger, D. (1991). Money meaning and madness: psychoanalytic perspective. *Psychoanalytic Review*, 78: 209–224.

Krueger, D. (1996). Money, success, and success phobia. In: D. W. Krueger (Ed.), *The Last Taboo: Money as Symbol and Reality in Psychotherapy and Psychoanalysis* (pp. 3–16). New York: Bruner/Mazel.

Lacan, J. (1966a). La direction de la cure et les principes de son pouvoir. In: *Ecrits II* (pp. 62–123). Paris: Editions du Seuil.

Lacan, J. (1966b). Le séminaire sur "La Lettre volée". In: *Ecrits I* (pp. 11–61). Paris: Editions du Seuil.

Lacan, J. (2013). *On the Names-of-the-Father.* Cambridge: Polity.

Laplanche, J., & Pontalis, J.-B. (1988). *The Language of Psychoanalysis.* London: Karnac.

Segal, H. (1989). Introduction. In: R. Britton, M. Feldman, & E. O'Shaughnessy (Eds.), *The Oedipus Complex Today: Clinical Implications* (pp. 00–00). London: Karnac.

Tuckett, D., & Taffler, T. (2008). Phantastic objects and the financial market's sense of reality: A psychoanalytic contribution to the understanding of stock market instability, *International Journal of Psychoanalysis* 89:389–412.

Wiseman, T. (1974). *The Money Motive: A Study of an Obsession.* London: Hutchinson.

Yablonsky, L. (1991). *The Emotional Meaning of Money.* London: Gardner Press.

Žižek, S. (2009). *First as Tragedy, then as Farce.* London: Verso.

CHAPTER ONE

Emotional functions of money

Anca Carrington

O f all the ways in which thinking about money can be approached, historical accounts have been, and remain, the most prolific. On this matter, De Quincey is mercilessly clear in spelling out the appeal of this solution: "Failing analytically to probe its nature, historically we seek relief to our perplexities by tracing its origin" (1893, p. 43). Most books on money turn away from unease and unanswered questions, and embrace instead classification and chronology (e.g., Eagleton & Williams, 2007). The majority of writers on this subject take great pleasure in listing the many forms in which money appeared over time, as it found itself embodied in coins or shells, knives, salt, axes, skins, iron, rice, mahogany, tobacco, paper, and, more recently, plastic, and electronic impulses. Even the recently refurbished Money Room at the British Museum does not offer much more than a striking but brief succession of eras and currencies, one swift move from shells to plastic, as if to say, with a nod and a wink, "Isn't money odd?" Yet, as Buchan (1997) puts it, while money is "of no particular substance at all" (pp. 17–18), in any given medium, and at any given time, money remains "incarnate desire" (p. 19), different and boundless for each person. It can at once convey and satisfy desire, even if only with a promise. Unlike other goods that can satisfy one desire at a time, money confronts not just one single need alone, but Need itself (Schopenhauer, cited in Buchan, 1997, p. 31).

Economics textbooks devote surprisingly little space to the nature of money, and focus instead on either elaborate policies that aim to manage money so that "more" takes the place of "less" in the relentless pursuit of economic growth, or complex financial techniques that can prove themselves so capable of generating such accumulation that little need for policy remains. As Galbraith (1975) rightly points out, "[T]he study of money, above all other fields in economics, is the one where complexity is used to disguise the truth or to evade the truth, not to reveal it" (p. 15), conveying the air of a Victorian novel about marriage that leaves out all mention of sex (Wiseman, 1974, p. 16). At the same time, as Buchan poignantly states, "whatever job it does, money does its job" (p. 182).

In the limited economics textbook space devoted to what money is and what it does, one learns something about the roles of money, as manifested in its functioning as means of exchange, unit of account, store of value, and, in some books, and some of the time, standard of deferred payment. The economics vocabulary also includes the concept of *money illusion*—not one usually uttered in public by policy makers. This refers to the tendency people have to think of money in nominal rather than in real (inflation-adjusted) terms. Disputed by some in terms of how much a policy-maker can rely on this being the case, I find this concept a highly insightful one, as we all know something about regarding money as capable of offering more than it can actually purchase.

I will explore each of the recognised functions of money in turn and posit that their universality and persistence in the external economy can be understood in terms of the corresponding internal economy on which these external functions map and in which they are anchored.

Money as means of exchange

As a means of exchange, money relies on its function as a measure of value, understood—in the vein of the prevailing rationalist view—as postulated on the basis of practical reason (Thomas, 2000). Money's ability to represent and measure value makes it a suitable device for separating the constraints of barter, where both parties must want the goods of the other and be prepared to exchange theirs for it. Thus, the barter scenario is

I has A
J has B
I wants B
J wants A
I and J swap A and B
I gets B
J gets A.

In the absence of money, I and J make either this transaction or none at all. By turning this dyad into a triangle, money makes it possible for the seller to turn buyer in a separate transaction, without being tied to what their buyer could offer. Thus,

I has money
I wants C
J has C
J wants E
I and J swap money and C
I gets C
J gets money
J swaps money for E (later, elsewhere).

In day-to-day exchanges, money is an impersonal vehicle for hidden but highly personal transactions, a mediator that provides the illusion of proximity without the cost of intimacy—it creates links with others, but not contact. A vivid depiction of this as-if-ness in the world of business and economics is provided by Galbraith (1975) who reminds us that

in monetary matters as in diplomacy, a nicely conformist nature, a good tailor and the ability to articulate the currently fashionable cliché have usually been better for personal success than an excessively inquiring mind. (p. 315)

In this way, money functions as facilitator of transactions not only in our conscious reality, but also—and arguably more so—in the unconscious domain, as what is being avoided on one level is constantly enacted on another. One's own relationship to money colours one's perception of how others might relate to it. It is on this level that money stands for what everyone desires, making any financial transaction a revolving Oedipal configuration, or what Green calls a "generalised triangulation with a substitutable third" (cited in Diatkine, 2007, p. 653). Having a lot of money can make one feel emotionally wealthy, the chosen one, iterated winner of a life-long oedipal dispute. This is a common phantasy, shared by the economically poor and rich alike. Money offers the promise to alleviate castration anxiety for men: in phantasy, wealth becomes equated with virility, making any woman accessible. For women, it can act as a means of denying the insurmountable gender divide, with the phallic woman either enjoying her experience of domination over the relatively poorer man, or feeling wary about putting suitors off by parading her status, under the spell of a powerful unconscious association between femininity and the underprivileged/castrated (Yablonsky, 1991).

Each transaction offers a pair of a triangular configurations linking, on the one hand, the seller, the buyer, and money, where the desired object for the seller is money as mediator, and, on the other hand, the seller, the buyer, and the purchased goods or service, where the desired object for the buyer is the goods or service purchased. This triangular configuration is endlessly self-generating, with the buyer in one transaction becoming seller and buyer in many others, and likewise for the initial seller.

As illustrated in Figure 1.1, the seller I has Dj, which is the buyer

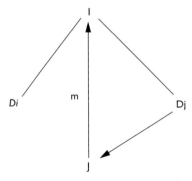

Figure 1.1.   The triangular transaction between a seller and a buyer, as mediated by money.

J's desired object. J gives I money (m) in exchange for Dj and I is now free to pursue his/her own desire, Di, through m. This configuration extends in all direction, in an expanding beehive of transactions that constitute a sort of molecular structure of the world economy.

Thus, each transaction offers the illusion of overcoming the oedipal barrier: the buyer (J at first) turns the inaccessible into accessible because s/he has the means (money) to get the desired object, with no obstacle in sight, as the rival (I) can be bought off and, thus, eliminated; the seller (I) acquires the means (money) that offers the promise of accessing his or her desired object in any future transaction with, say, K, as well as a replenishment of virility. As Yablonsky (1991) explores in detail, "both sexes are responsible for the perpetration of this money/virility myth" (p. 33).

If we were to apply this configuration to the payment of fees in psychoanalysis, it is easy to see how the patient bypasses others in the analyst's life by paying for the analytic hour, accessing in this way—albeit temporarily—the dual relationship of phantasy; at the same time, the analyst gives up the hour, and other pursuits of desire that continue to exist beyond the confines of the session. An element of residual frustration about the limited power of money to secure such exclusivity characterises all transactions, but, in the particular exchange of therapy, this can be, and often is, addressed and explored.

Money as unit of account

As unit of account, money acts as a standardised unit of measurement across transactions. In the examples above, A, B, and so on had their own monetary value, m(A), m(B), etc. In the case of barter,

> I has A
> J has B
> I wants B
> J wants A
> I and J swap A and B
> I gets B
> J gets A,

we could argue that I values B more than J does, and J values A more than I does. When they make the exchange, each makes a gain by obtaining something they value more than what they had to start with. With money in place,

I has money
I wants C
J has C
J wants E
I and J swap money and C
I gets C
J gets money
J swaps money for E (later, elsewhere),

the buyer I pays m(C), some of which is then turned later by J into m(E). Although I parts with m(C) and J parts with C, arguably I values C more than m(C) in order to pursue the exchange. The same is true for J and his desired object, E. Also, J also values m(C) more than C, parting with C for the money that can be then used to obtain E.

Economics alone would propose that A=B in barter or C=m(C) in the money economy, or else the first exchange either would not take place, or an adjustment would occur in the prices and/or quantities until the exchange can occur in the moneyed economy. My argument is that it is the added internal sense of value and emotional investment (cathexis) that makes such exchanges worth pursuing. In other words, desire. Something about exchange and personal value attributed to goods or services is dealt with in mainstream economics, ironically enough using the concept of *"indifference* curves" to capture an assumed equivalence of preferences for the same level of "utility". Yet, the entire exercise is as far from indifference as it can be, and definitely not purely utilitarian.

The one domain where the experience of this exchange has been the most explored psychoanalytically is that of the financial transactions between therapist and patient, around the issue of psychoanalytic fees and their payment in private practice. The focus of this literature is rather narrow, as it remains dominated by a specific set of themes: the presence or absence of fees and their the impact on the analytic experience (mostly in terms of associated resistance patterns), the level of fees and its relationship to the patient's financial circumstances (from very poor to extremely wealthy), change in the financial circumstances of the patient during analysis, and changing the level of fees, payment for missed sessions, missed payment, and the collection of debt, payment by third parties, and the mechanics of the monetary transactions between patient and therapist (see Krueger, 1986 for a comprehensive coverage of these issues). Underpinning these themes is an unspoken assumption that the patient is endlessly fragile on all matters related to money and that, somehow, the impact of this on the analysis should be minimised rather than this being, alongside everything else, open to questioning and enquiry. By implication, analysts themselves are assumed to be invulnerable to such matters. Against the background of a detailed overview of these themes, Eissler (1974) recognises, with some degree of timidity, that analysts themselves cannot always keep their own attitudes towards money free from "irrational infusion" and that "a veil of unintended secrecy" covers the triangular formation of the analyst, fee, and patient. Also, in passing, he notes that psychoanalysis itself evolved, in historico-sociological terms, in conjunction with finance capitalism, offering, as it were, something from and for the wealthy and the upper middle class. Although he does not explore the consequences of this, it is as if he offers a possible explanation for the persistent reluctance in the profession to question this very history and its possible meaning.

Famously labelled by Krueger (1986) as "the last emotional taboo" (p. vii), the issue of money in psychoanalysis retains the quality of a "fiscal blind spot" (Weissberg, 1989). What seems to complicate the matter and compromise the availability of ordinary psychoanalytic thinking and insight is the very economic dependence of therapists on their patients. It is interesting to note that the decade that generated a wave of publications deploring "the striking paucity of discussions about the meaning of money" (Rothstein, 1986, p. 299) in psychotherapy was the 1980s, a time of visible increase in wealth and disparities in the western world, where the open and aggressive pursuit of money was a defining feature of society. It was as if the analytic profession was both wishing to catch up with this wave, and resentful of being unable to, because of the bounds that the nature of their work imposed on them. Perhaps it is no coincidence for this book to mark a return to thinking psychoanalytically about money, at a time when the recent global financial crises have left none of us unaffected and money has returned as cause for concern, this time provoking with its fragility rather than its promising abundance.

The recurrent discussion around the setting of the level of fees and their possible adjustment in relation to the patient's financial circumstances reveals something about the lack of clarity and the discomfort some therapists have around the value they place on their own time and skills, especially as the issue of fees is also absent from most trainings (Lasky, 1984; Shields, 1996), thus perpetuating an avoidant stance. This resonates with Yablonsky's (1991) finding that the positions of entrepreneur and helper that psychotherapists find themselves in are often in conflict, whereby "An inner tug of war ensues between idealism and humanitarianism on the one hand and materialism on the other" (p. 158), or what Krueger (1986) describes as "the antipodes of altruism and self-interest" (p. ix). Liss-Levinson (1990) proposes that this problem is more pronounced in the case of women analysts, who struggle more than men with the tension between the needs of the self and the needs of the other, as she explores findings that, overall, women analysts have lower fees.

Furthermore, as Freud (1917e) has famously put it, "People never willingly abandon a libidinal position, not even, indeed, when a substitute is already beckoning to them" (p. 244). This offers insight into money's attractiveness as an element of continuity, as well as into the asymmetric way in which we perceive a gain and a loss of equal monetary value. As a simple illustration, note the common experience of unease and disorientation that using foreign currency triggers, as well as the underlying belief of the traveller of "his own money at home to be privileged and natural and all others to be departures from it, as all languages from his mother tongue" (Buchan, 1997, p. 190).

It is, I hope, becoming clearer how money is not only the currency of our daily shopping, but also that of daily complex and mostly hidden emotional transactions. The functions it performs in the external economy have their internal, unconscious counterpart, and the experience of each individual transaction links in complex ways with a shared and unspoken space of symbolism and meaning. The symbolic function of money has long been recognised. Buchan quotes Hodges, an eighteenth-century English historian, who, in 1697, conveyed this very idea succinctly and with poetic beauty:

> The value of money has been settled by general consent to express our wants and our property, as letters were invented to express our ideas; and both these inventions, by giving more active energy to the powers

and passions of human nature, have contributed to multiply the objects they were designed to represent. (1997, p. 20)

The world of money has become increasingly one of endless oscillation between continuity and discontinuity, shaped by divisibility, fungibility, and countability, whereby things can be turned into fractions, exchanged for each other, can be separated at one time and brought together at another, done and undone, damaged and repaired. This is very much the landscape of the internal phantasy, where whole and part-objects reside, where transformations have the fluidity of dream, yet true change can be avoided and repetition without alteration is possible, alive, and endless.

Economists use the label of "purchasing power" to designate the amount of real goods and services that can be bought with each unit of money (Black, 1997, p. 381), but it is the power of money in phantasy, with its quality of omnipotence, that gives it such unshakeable importance in our lives.

Money as store of value

As the world economy hovers on either side of the official definition of recession, the media abounds with stories of staggering lottery wins. I find that, at my current pay rate, close to the UK average in 2011, I would need to work 2,187 years to earn as much as one such recently claimed and publicised prize. On the same front page of this "free" London daily (*Metro*, 10 February 2012), one finds an article about the lead actor in the Harry Potter films, a series that has earned 150 times more than the lottery win on which my first calculation was based. The twenty-two-year-old is quoted as saying, "Money? It does not motivate me." I ask myself, what does this mean? About my sense of value? Freedom? Desire? Hope? Tolerance? And, likewise, about his.

De-materialisation moved money into a territory where everything is possible. Now, money exists in the overlapping zone between real and symbolic, in the ordinary rather than the Lacanian sense, where a great degree of cross-contamination is both possible and invited. This is the place where the symbolic can be treated as real, and the real as symbolic. To illustrate the former, think of how money continued to perform its task long after the gold parity was eliminated and the printed paper issued by banks stopped having its touchable counterpart in some inaccessible but existing vault. To visualise the latter, think of how the power of mathematical artefacts applied to virtual money ruled in the run-up to the latest financial crisis and still defines job descriptions for well-paid jobs in the undeterred world of finance. Indeed, the latest addition to the monetary domain, the Bitcoin, is "a new specie" (*The Economist*, 2013a), a purely mathematically generated, decentralised digital currency, underpinned by peer-to-peer computer networking rather than by a central monetary authority (*The Economist*, 2013b).

This particular aspect, of the role of the issuing authority in establishing the credibility and validity of money, carries great weight in the symbolic domain—understood in both the ordinary and the Lacanian senses. The right to issue money is a highly privileged one, the entitlement of kings and, more recently, the state. Indeed, the economic concept of *seigniorage* captures something of this archaic but powerful order, as it refers to a source of revenue based on the very right to issue money, and is defined as "The profits made by a ruler from issuing money", and related originally to "the profits from the issue of coinage with a face value greater than its cost of production" (Black, 1997, p. 421). In other words, it is the economic measure of the power of law invested in the issuing authority.

In the Oedipus myth itself, the killed father is no ordinary man, but the king—presumably the richest man in the land. Taking his life means not only taking his wife, but also the accompanying material riches, including the right to issue money, one would imagine. This aspect of the myth remains as powerful as the rest. Schindler (1983) proposes that money is "frequently in the eyes of the child a sign of father's omnipotence" and that economic development "is influenced to a great extent by the father–son relationship as part of the Oedipus complex" (p. 72). Tracking the evolution of values in society, Saroldi (2002) deplores the current era, where she perceives that "the function of the father as Lawgiver is supplanted by the function of money as the only value and measure of all things" (p. 209).

The boundary between the symbolic and the real domain is a porous one, fizzy with constant movement. As Buchan (1997) beautifully puts it,

> Money is one of those human creations that make concrete a sensation, in this case the sensation of wanting, as a clock does the sensation of passing time. It is that double aspect of money, airy and substantial, that fascinated all civilisations. (p. 269)

The porosity of this barrier is what made possible the emergence and acceptance of increasingly sophisticated financial products, invested from the start with attributes of a phantastic object (see Chapter Four).

Before moving deeper into the internal economy, a quick return to money in its old-fashioned, material manifestations. Coins and banknotes out of circulation return, after a while, to the realm of commodity, and become subject to transaction like any other historical objects, joining the circuit of antiques and collectables, old money changing hands for new, dead currency swapping place with living currency at auctions, gathered and dispersed again by collectors and specialist traders. Left outside this circuit, obsolete money fades relentlessly into uselessness, as Buchan (1997) vividly conveys as he reminisces about banknotes he kept in a drawer after they went out of circulation: "I kept them because I sensed their value evaporating, their moneyness seeping into the old satinwood, till they were just coloured paper you couldn't even write on" (p. 12).

Banknotes currently in circulation, once they become worn out or damaged, retire and get turned into briquettes used as agricultural compost (BBC, 2012), an aptly Freudian exit. One of the arguments put forward in the same radio show was that we believe in money because it works. A necessary, but not sufficient, condition. The converse, that money works because we believe in it or, rather, does not when we do not believe in it, becomes most apparent during every financial crisis. The recent one has brought a real change to all of us: an increase in wealth to a few, a loss of assets and increase in debt and hopelessness to most, but also a symbolic change, as the ever-crumbling trust in the euro between 2010 and 2012 shows. Like unappeased gods, the markets demolished by night what Brussels policy-makers tried to put back together by day. It might well be that the fragility of the trust in this particular project, of the new European currency, stems in part from our witnessing its creation, from it being not so much an inherited myth, but one we watched being put together and failed to believe in as a consequence.

Berger (1972) provides a poignant emotional definition of money:

Money is life. Not in the sense that without money you starve. Not in the sense that capital gives one class power over the entire lives of another class. But in the sense that *money is a token of, and the key to, every human capacity*. The power to spend money is the power to live. According to the legends of publicity, those who lack the power to spend money become literally *faceless*. Those who have the power become *lovable*. (p. 137, my italics)

On a psychic level, money stores not any odd value, but that of our very existence. As the money phantasies explored by Wiseman (1974) show, we use it as both a defence against the pain of not feeling loved, and as means of punishing those whose desire rests elsewhere. Where the punishment of others takes the form of attacks in phantasy on the internal objects, money offers the solution by facilitating buying as an act of reparation. In this sense, money is not just a store of value, but a restorer if it. Furthermore, as the exploration of childhood phantasies in Chapter Three shows, money is invested early on with the power to negotiate an easy bypassing of emotional deprivation and loss and to allow the acquisition in phantasy of what is painfully lacking in reality. The geometry of the oedipal configuration, with its negotiation by external transactions, is in place almost from the start.

What becomes of this in adult life is well captured in a story that shimmers with the richness of this interplay between the individual and the collective and between the symbolic and the real—Mark Twain's story of 1893, "The £1,000,000 bank-note", first published in 1893. (The Bank of England has, in fact, been using £1 million notes since the eighteenth century for the purpose of internal accounting. The entrance to the Bank of England Museum is adorned with an oversized such banknote, signed by the Queen in December 2012, presumably not for accounting purposes, but as a display of what power and authority can achieve with its stamp even in times of financial crisis.)

In Twain's story, the protagonist, following a bet between rich men, unknown to him, is given just such an extraordinary banknote to spend. Nobody is in a position to give him the change to any of his purchases, so they sell him everything on credit, expecting future payment which, they believe, a man of his means could not fail to make. Without spending any actual money, the previously destitute man, buys food and shelter, and, most of all, a reputation for wealth—which he can even lend to friends by vouching for their business reliability—and, ultimately, a wife. What is most remarkable in this short and entertaining tale is the clarity with which the impact of money (both actual and potential, both real and imaginary) has on how the character sees himself and is seen by others. His bewilderment and struggle to stick to what he knew of himself from before is at odds with how others see him, which is almost exclusively through this extraordinary and external aspect of his circumstances. But even the main character himself, who remains nameless throughout, becomes gradually unable to see his own identity other than as defined by the way he responds to the surprising circumstances he finds himself in. Money becomes a sort of double-sided mirror that reflects any interaction he has with himself and with others, whether they know the story behind his extraordinary fortune or not. While, in a sense, the sudden riches are not real, once they are accepted as such, he becomes able to get involved in real business and accumulate real earnings. The promise of money generates more money, and credit is entirely dependent on the strength of the shared belief and convention.

That this is still the case more than 100 years on is well captured by Žižek's (2009) analysis of the global response to the financial crisis that defined the first decade of the twenty-first century:

> let us not forget that the sublimely enormous sums of money were spent not on some clear 'real' or concrete problem, but essentially in order to *restore confidence* in the markets, that is, simply to change people's beliefs. (p. 80)

In a sense, the need to sustain a symbol becomes more real than the reality of other, arguably fundamental, needs. The price is a high one, as $318 was spent on buying trust at a time of financial crisis in 2009 for every $1 spent on alleviating famine, which affected close to one billion people in 2010 (World Hunger Education Service, 2013). In the case of the lengthy euro crisis that marked this decade, over one trillion euro (i.e., 1,000 billion, or £847 billion) had been spent by the European Central Bank on "saving the euro" by February 2012 (*Evening Standard*, 2012), compared to an annual European budget of fifty billion euro for international aid, so a ratio of a 20:1 between belief and starvation. Žižek (2009) links money to the relationship between symptom and fetish, where the former is the place where the repressed erupts, while the latter functions as "the embodiment of the lie which enables us to sustain the unbearable truth" (p. 65), in the split between disavowed beliefs and a remainder reality that, thus, becomes bearable.

Money as a standard of deferred payment

As a standard of deferred payment, money is the accepted way of settling a debt and the unit in which this debt is denominated. The advent of credit, replacing metal with faith, enhanced, rather than diminished, the place of money in the domain of desire and phantasy. This was recognised and articulated by Hodges, who explains that the

> whole Value that is put upon Money by Mankind, speaking generally, is extrinsick to the Money, and hath its real seat in those good things, through the Estimation providentially put upon it, which it is capable to purchase. (1697, p. 147, cited in Buchan, 1997, p. 104)

Yet, less than a hundred years later, Adam Smith, founding father of economics, as he is known, disregarded the place of emotions where money is concerned and asserted that what it conveys is not wishes, but thoughts, and that people pursue, accumulate, and spend money under the guide of rationality and always with benign effects. (The wish within the discipline of economics to be taken seriously and regarded as a science was such that "[i]n the two centuries after Smith, more mental effort was wasted objectifying his system of belief than on any other in history, not excluding the immortality of the soul and the rentability of civilian nuclear power" (Buchan, 1997, p. 178).)

Rationality is fighting its own battle in economics, where too many challenges to it have now been raised to be ignored—see, for example, the Institute for New Economic Thinking, INET (http://inet economics.org/) for the new home of economics, one hopes not in exile.

One much deferred payment was that of attention to the issue of money in the internal world and the relationship this bears to the external one, in which this book itself aims to become an object of desire and be sold at a price, so that the authors themselves can be freed to pursue other desires of their own. Far from being the last psychoanalytic word on money, this is, rather, intended as the beginning of a rigorous debate that is asking to take shape and to which psychoanalytic thinking can make a unique contribution.

References

BBC (2012). *Analysis: What Is Money?* Radio 4 broadcast, 26 March.

Berger, J. (1972). *Ways of Seeing*. London: Penguin Books.

Black, J. (1997). *Dictionary of Economics*. Oxford: Oxford University Press.

Buchan, J. (1997). *Frozen Desire: An Inquiry into the Meaning of Money*. London: Picador.

De Quincey, T. (1893). Style: part II. In: *Essays on Style, Rhetoric and Language*, Boston, MA: FN Scott.

Diatkine, G. (2007). Lacan. *International Journal of Psychoanalysis, 88*: 643–660.

Eagleton, C., & Williams, J. (2007). *Money: A History* (2nd edn). London: British Museum Press.

Eissler, K. R. (1974). On some theoretical and technical problems regarding the payment of fees for psychoanalytic treatment. *International Journal of Psychoanalysis, 1*(1–2): 73–101.

Evening Standard (2012). ECB bailout for banks tops 1trn in cheap loans rush. Available at: www.standard.co.uk/business/business-news/ecb-bailout-for-banks-tops-1trn-in-cheap-loans-rush-7498362.html.

Freud, S. (1917e). Mourning and melancholia. *S.E., 14*: 239–258. London: Hogarth.

Galbraith, J. K. (1975). *Money: Whence It Came, Where It Went*. Harmondsworth: Penguin.

Hodges, J. (1697). *The Present State of England as to Coin and Publick Charges*. London: Andr. Bell.

Krueger, D. W. (Ed.) (1986). *The Last Taboo: Money as Symbol and Reality in Psychotherapy and Psychoanalysis*. New York: Bruner/Mazel.

Lasky, E. (1984). Psychoanalysts' and psychotherapists' conflicts about setting fees. *Psychoanalytic Psychology, 1*(4): 289–300.

Liss-Levinson, N. (1990). Money matters and the woman analyst: in a different voice. *Psychoanalytic Psychology, 7*(Suppl.): 119–130.

Rothstein, A. (1986). The seduction of money: a brief note on an expression of transference love. *Psychoanalytic Quarterly, 55*: 296–300.

Saroldi, N. (2002). Do we still have anything to do with the old blind man? *International Forum of Psychoanalysis, 11*(3): 209–214.

Schindler, W. (1983). Economic Oedipus complex: the libidinal aspects of economic strength. *International Journal of Social Psychiatry, 29*: 68–72.

Shields, J. D. (1996). Hostage to the fee: meanings of money, counter-transference, and the beginning therapist. *Psychoanalytic Psychotherapy*, 10(3): 233–250.

The Economist (2013a). A new specie. Available at: www.economist.com/news/leaders/21576104-regulators-should-keep-their-hands-new-forms-digital-money-such-bitcoin-new-specie.

The Economist (2013b). *The Economist* explains: How does Bitcoin work. Available at: www.economist.com.blogs/economist-explains/2013/04/economist-explains-how-does-bitcoin-work.

Thomas, A. (2000). Values. In: *Concise Routledge Encyclopedia of Philosophy*. London: Routledge.

Twain, M. (1893). The £1,000,000 bank-note. In: *The Complete Short Stories of Mark Twain*. New York: Bantam Books.

Weissberg, J. H. (1989). The fiscal blind spot in psychotherapy. *Journal of the American Academy of Psychoanalysis*, 17(3): 475–482.

Wiseman, T. (1974). *The Money Motive: A Study of an Obsession*. London: Hutchinson.

World Hunger Education Service (2013). 2013 World hunger and poverty facts and statistics. Available at: www.worldhunger.org/articles/Learn/world%20hunger%20facts%202002.htm.

Yablonsky, L. (1991). *The Emotional Meaning of Money*. London: Gardner Press.

Žižek, S. (2009). *First as Tragedy, then as Farce*. London: Verso.

CHAPTER TWO

Freud's papers on money

Anca Carrington

Introduction

Freud's seminal paper of 1908(b) is a short contribution, a "communication", as he describes it, rooted in clinical observation rather than in theoretical preconception. Yet, the argument is sketchy and remains unsubstantiated by clinical material, in a way that gives it the quality of a note to himself, but one that he was in a hurry to share with his readers. Something about this rushed quality might be understood in terms of his own personal unease around money. Warner (1989) explores Freud's personal relationship to money, his struggle to manage his financial responsibility, his inclination to borrow more money than he repaid, his resentment towards being in debt, as well as his discomfort at the thought of poverty, linked, as this was, in his mind with his father's "generous improvidence" (p. 609). There is something about this personal dimension, about this apparent mix of deprivation and entitlement, that perhaps made it difficult for Freud to retain his usual inquisitiveness around difficult questions, and prevented him from becoming more involved psychoanalytically with money and its role in the unconscious. The review of Freud's correspondence, and of the subsequent literature on the fortunes of the

Freud family provided by Warner, indicate that Freud was troubled more by an internal sense of deprivation than by one of actual destitution. This is described by what Drucker (1978), an economist acquainted with the Freud family, called a "poorhouse neurosis", which, in his view, prevented Freud from addressing money openly in his work in the way he did address sexuality. It is, in fact, in this oblique way, through an exploration of sexuality and erotism, that Freud makes his first contribution on the subject of money.

Thus, the focus of his attention in the 1908 paper is the relationship between early bodily experience and mental development, as seen in the connection between the character traits of orderliness, parsimony, and obstinacy found in adults and the childhood inclination to control their stools as a source of pleasure, in those displaying them. Freud links this inclination to an innate heightened erotogenicity of the anal zone which, in the course of development, either continues sexually, or is transformed into such character traits, either by sublimation or reaction formation. He explores the relationship between money and faeces through quick cultural references, and understands their identification in the unconscious mind to be based on the very contrast between them in terms of value: "most precious substance", and "refuse". Ferenczi (1916) expands Freud's idea that *money = faeces*, exploring the gradual sublimation process that accompanies development and showing how differences in the blend of transformed and unprocessed parts can lead to "the most variegated character types", from entrepreneurs to artists, and positing that capitalism is securely anchored into the satisfaction of the pleasure principle. In a return to Ferenczi's contribution, Haight (1977) explores the reality of crapitalism from a philosophical perspective, as he explores the "four-letter word" status of money in society. This remains apt, in view of the perpetuating prudishness with which Freud's ideas are still received, even by contemporary readers. At the same time, the *money = faeces* identity can be regarded as an established dictum in the analytic profession, with "miserliness firmly ensconced as an anal trait" (Akhtar, 2009, p. 70).

As Borneman (1976) points out, the crux of understanding this view on the anality of money "lies in the observation that feces is the child's first autonomous product, its first 'possession'", with the "child's discovery of the self and of its power over its surroundings" occurring as "concurrent events" (p. 3).

In this paper, Freud mentions the existence of a "money complex", but does not define this or elaborate on its genesis and evolution. Yet, the concept of "complex" holds the key to the fundamental importance of money, given that it designates an "organised group of ideas and memories of great affective force which are either partly or totally unconscious" and which are "constituted on the basis of interpersonal relationships of childhood history" (Laplanche & Pontalis, 1988, p. 72).

By 1917, Freud uses anal erotism as an illustration of a wider idea that his earlier paper began to capture: that of a theoretical understanding of the transformations undergone by instincts in the process of development. He takes as fact that the concepts of faeces (money, gift), baby, and penis are treated in the unconscious as equivalent, basing his belief on his analysis of the dreams of adult patients, and of symbolic speech which does not differentiate between sexes. Yet, as Chapter Three shows, this fluidity is visibly present in childhood, especially around the age of toilet training and exploration of the differences between sexes.

This second paper (1917c) coveys a sense of urgency, as well as one of frustration, in Freud's effort to map and explain the complex interconnections that the unconscious mind finds so easy to navigate. He even includes a diagram, which is the exception rather than the norm as far as his writing style is concerned. The sense of underlying impatience is similar to that in the first (1908b) paper. Nevertheless, these two brief contributions provide the solid foundation on which a psychoanalytic understanding of money and its role in our internal lives can rest.

The notes to the text are as presented in the *Standard Edition*, with those in square brackets belonging to the editor, James Strachey, and the rest to Freud.

References

Akhtar, S. (2009). *Turning Points in Dynamic Psychotherapy: Initial Assessment, Boundaries, Money, Disruptions and Suicidal Crises*. London: Karnac.

Borneman, E. (1976). *The Psychoanalysis of Money*. New York: Urizen Books.

Drucker, P. F. (1978). *Adventures of a Bystander*. New York: Harper and Row.

Ferenczi, S. (1916). The ontogenesis of the interest in money. In: *Contributions to Psychoanalysis* (pp. 269–279). Toronto: Richard G. Badger.

Freud, S. (1908b). Character and anal erotism. *S.E.*, *9*: 169–175. London: Hogarth.

Freud, S. (1917c). On transformations of instinct as exemplified in anal erotism. *S.E.*, *17*: 125–134. London: Hogarth.

Haight, D. F. (1977). Is money a four-letter word? *Psychoanalytic Review*, *64*(4): 621–629.

Laplanche, J., & Pontalis, J.-B. (1988). *The Language of Psychoanalysis*, D. Nicholson-Smith (Trans.). London: Karnac.

Warner, S. (1989). Sigmund Freud and money. *Journal of the American Academy of Psychoanalysis*, *17*(4): 609–622.

Freud (1908a): Character and anal erotism*

Among those whom we try to help by our psycho-analytic efforts we often come across a type of person who is marked by the possession of a certain set of character-traits, while at the same time our attention is drawn to the behaviour in his childhood of one of his bodily functions and the organ concerned in it. I cannot say at this date what particular occasions began to give me an impression that there was some organic connection between this type of character and this behaviour of an organ, but I can assure the reader that no theoretical expectation played any part in that impression.

Accumulated experience has so much strengthened my belief in the existence of such a connection that I am venturing to make it the subject of a communication.

The people I am about to describe are noteworthy for a regular combination of the three following characteristics. They are especially *orderly, parsimonious* and *obstinate*. Each of these words actually covers a small group or series of interrelated character-traits. "Orderly"[1] covers the notion of bodily cleanliness, as well as of conscientiousness

---

* Freud, S. (1908a). Character and anal erotism. *S.E., 9.*

in carrying out small duties and trustworthiness. Its opposite would be "untidy" and "neglectful". Parsimony may appear in the exaggerated form of avarice; and obstinacy can go over into defiance, to which rage and revengefulness are easily joined. The two latter qualities – parsimony and obstinacy – are linked with each other more closely than they are with the first – with orderliness. They are, also, the more constant element of the whole complex. Yet it seems to me incontestable that all three in some way belong together.

It is easy to gather from these people's early childhood history that they took a comparatively long time to overcome their infantile *incontinentia alvi* [faecal incontinence], and that even in later childhood they suffered from isolated failures of this function. As infants, they seem to have belonged to the class who refuse to empty their bowels when they are put on the pot because they derive a subsidiary pleasure from defaecating;[2] for they tell us that even in somewhat later years they enjoyed holding back their stool, and they remember – though more readily about their brothers and sisters than about themselves – doing all sorts of unseemly things with the faeces that had been passed. From these indications we infer that such people are born with a sexual constitution in which the erotogenicity of the anal zone is exceptionally strong. But since none of these weaknesses and idiosyncrasies are to be found in them once their childhood has been passed, we must conclude that the anal zone had lost its erotogenic significance in the course of development; and it is to be suspected that the regularity with which this triad of properties is present in their character may be brought into relation with the disappearance of their anal erotism.

I know that no one is prepared to believe in a state of things so long as it appears to be unintelligible and to offer no angle from which an explanation can be attempted. But we can at least bring the underlying factors nearer to our understanding by the help of the postulates I laid down in my Three Essays on the Theory of Sexuality in 1905.[3] I there attempted to show that the sexual instinct of man is highly complex and is put together from contributions made by numerous constituents and component instincts. Important contributions to "sexual excitation" are furnished by the peripheral excitations of certain specially designated parts of the body (the genitals, mouth, anus, urethra), which therefore deserve to be described as "erotogenic zones". But the amounts of excitation coming in from these parts of the body do not all undergo the same vicissitudes, nor is the fate of all of them the same at every period of life. Generally speaking, only a part of them is made use of in sexual life; another part is deflected from sexual aims and directed towards others – a process which deserves the name of "sublimation". During the period of life which may be called the period of "sexual latency" – i.e. from the completion of the fifth year[4] to the first manifestations of puberty (round about the eleventh year) – reaction-formations, or counter-forces, such as shame, disgust and morality, are created in the mind. They are actually formed at the expense of the excitations proceeding from the erotogenic zones, and they rise like dams to oppose the later activity of the sexual instincts. Now anal erotism is one of the components of the [sexual] instinct which, in the course of development and in accordance with the education demanded by our present civilisation, have become unserviceable for sexual aims. It is therefore plausible to suppose that these character-traits of orderliness, parsimony and obstinacy, which are so often prominent in people who were formerly anal erotics, are to be regarded as the first and most constant results of the sublimation of anal erotism.[5]

The intrinsic necessity for this connection is not clear, of course, even to myself. But I can make some suggestions which may help towards an understanding of it. Cleanliness, orderliness and trustworthiness give exactly the impression of a reaction-formation against an interest in what is unclean and disturbing and should not be part of the body. ("Dirt is matter in the wrong place.")[6] To relate obstinacy to an interest in defecation would seem no easy task; but it should be remembered that even babies can show self-will about parting with their stool, as we have seen above, and that it is a general practice in children's upbringing to administer painful stimuli to the skin of the buttocks – which is linked up with the erotogenic anal zone – in order to break their obstinacy and make them submissive. An invitation to a caress of the anal zone is still used to-day, as it was in ancient times, to express defiance or defiant scorn, and thus in reality signifies an act of tenderness that has been overtaken by repression. An exposure of the buttocks represents a softening down of this spoken invitation into a gesture; in Goethe's *Götz von Berlichingen* both words and gesture are introduced at the most appropriate point as an expression of defiance.[7]

The connections between the complexes of interest in money and of defecation, which seem so dissimilar, appear to be the most extensive of all. Every doctor who has practised psycho-analysis knows that the most refractory and long-standing cases of what is described as habitual constipation in neurotics can be cured by that form of treatment. This is less surprising if we remember that that function has shown itself similarly amenable to hypnotic suggestion. But in psycho-analysis one only achieves this result if one deals with the patients' money complex and induces them to bring it into consciousness with all its connections. It might be supposed that the neurosis is here only following an indication of common usage in speech, which calls a person who keeps too careful a hold on his money "dirty" or "filthy".[8] But this explanation would be far too superficial. In reality, wherever archaic modes of thought have predominated or persist – in the ancient civilisations, in myths, fairy tales and superstitions, in unconscious thinking, in dreams and in neuroses – money is brought into the most intimate relationship with dirt. We know that the gold which the devil gives his paramours turns into excrement after his departure, and the devil is certainly nothing else than the personification of the repressed unconscious instinctual life.[9] We also know about the superstition which connects the finding of treasure with defecation,[10] and everyone is familiar with the figure of the "shitter of ducats [Dukatenscheisser]".[11] Indeed, even according to ancient Babylonian doctrine gold is "the faeces of Hell" (Mammon = *ilu manman*[12]). Thus in following the usage of language, neurosis, here as elsewhere, is taking words in their original, significant sense, and where it appears to be using a word figuratively it is usually simply restoring its old meaning.[13]

It is possible that the contrast between the most precious substance known to men and the most worthless, which they reject as waste matter ("refuse"[14]), has led to this specific identification of gold with faeces.

Yet another circumstance facilitates this equation in neurotic thought. The original erotic interest in defecation is, as we know, destined to be extinguished in later years. In those years the interest in money makes its appearance as a new interest which had been absent in childhood. This makes it easier for the earlier impulsion, which is in process of losing its aim, to be carried over to the newly emerging aim.

If there is any basis in fact for the relation posited here between anal erotism and this triad of character-traits, one may expect to find no very marked degree of "anal character" in people who have retained the anal zone's erotogenic character in adult life, as happens, for instance, with certain homosexuals. Unless I am much mistaken, the evidence of experience tallies quite well on the whole with this inference.

We ought in general to consider whether other character-complexes, too, do not exhibit a connection with the excitations of particular erotogenic zones. At present I only know of the intense "burning" ambition of people who earlier suffered from enuresis.[15] We can at any rate lay down a formula for the way in which character in its final shape is formed out of the constituent instincts: the permanent character-traits are either unchanged prolongations of the original instincts, or sublimations of those instincts, or reaction-formations against them.[16]

Notes

1. ["*Ordentlich*" in German. The original meaning of the word is "orderly"; but it has become greatly extended in use. It can be the equivalent of such English terms as "correct", "tidy", "cleanly", "trustworthy", as well as "regular", "decent" and "proper", in the more colloquial senses of those words.]
2. Cf. Freud, *Three Essays on the Theory of Sexuality* (1905d), S.E., 7, p. 186.
3. [The material in the present paragraph is derived mainly from Section 5 of the first essay and Section 1 of the second (*Standard Ed.*, 7, 167 ff. and 176 ff.).]
4. [In the German editions before 1924 this read "from the completion of the fourth year".]
5. Since it is precisely the remarks in my *Three Essays on the Theory of Sexuality* about the anal erotism of infants that have particularly scandalised uncomprehending readers, I venture at this point to interpolate an observation for which I have to thank a very intelligent patient. "A friend of mine", he told me, "who has read your *Three Essays on the Theory of Sexuality*, was talking about the book. He entirely agreed with it, but there was one passage, which – though of course he accepted and understood its meaning like that of the rest – struck him as so grotesque and comic that he sat down and laughed over it for a quarter of an hour. This passage ran: 'One of the clearest signs of subsequent eccentricity or nervousness is to be seen when a baby obstinately refuses to empty his bowels when he is put on the pot – that is, when his nurse wants him to – and holds back that function till he himself chooses to exercise it. He is

naturally not concerned with dirtying the bed, he is only anxious not to miss the subsidiary pleasure attached to defecating.' [*Standard Ed., 7,* p. 186.] The picture of this baby sitting on the pot and deliberating whether he would put up with a restriction of this kind upon his personal freedom of will, and feeling anxious, too, not to miss the pleasure attached to defecating, – this caused my friend the most intense amusement. About twenty minutes afterwards, as we were having some cocoa, he suddenly remarked without any preliminary: 'I say, seeing the cocoa in front of me has suddenly made me think of an idea that I always had when I was a child. I used always to pretend to myself that I was the cocoa-manufacturer Van Houten' (he pronounced the name Van 'Hauten' [i.e. with the first syllable rhyming with the English word 'cow']) 'and that I possessed a great secret for the manufacture of this cocoa. Everybody was trying to get hold of this secret that was a boon to humanity but I kept it carefully to myself. I don't know why I should have hit specially upon Van Houten. Probably his advertisements impressed me more than any others.' Laughing, and without thinking at the time that my words had any deep meaning, I said: "Wann haut'n die Mutter?' ['When does mother smack?' The first two words in the German phrase are pronounced exactly like 'Van Houten'.] It was only later that I realized that my pun in fact contained the key to the whole of my friend's sudden childhood recollection, and I then recognised it as a brilliant example of a screen-phantasy. My friend's phantasy, while keeping to the situation actually involved (the nutritional process) and making use of phonetic associations ('Kakao' ['cocoa'. – 'Kaka' is the common German nursery word for 'faeces' – cf. a dream at the end of Section IX of Freud, 1923c] and 'Wann haut'n'), pacified his sense of guilt by making a complete reversal in the content of his recollection: there was a displacement from the back of the body to the front, excreting food became taking food in, and something that was shameful and had to be concealed became a secret that was a boon to humanity. I was interested to see how, only a quarter of an hour after my friend had fended the phantasy off (though, it is true, in the comparatively mild form of raising an objection on formal grounds), he was, quite involuntarily, presented with the most convincing evidence by his own unconscious."

6. [This sentence is in English in the original.]
7. [The scene occurs in Act III, when Götz is summoned by a Herald to surrender. In the later acting version of the play the words are toned down.]
8. [The English "filthy" as well as the German "*filzig*" appears in the original. Freud had already commented on the usage mentioned here, in a

letter to Fliess of December 22, 1897 (Freud, 1950, Letter 79) and, later, in the first edition of *The Interpretation of Dreams* (1900), *Standard Ed.*, *4*, 200.]

9. Compare hysterical possession and demoniac epidemics. [Freud discussed this at considerable length in Part III of his paper "A seventeenth century demonological neurosis" (1923a). The legendary transformation of witches' gold into faeces and the comparison with the *"Dukatenscheisser"* below had already been mentioned by Freud in a letter to Fliess of January 24, 1897 (1950, Letter 57).]

10. [Numerous examples of this derived from folklore are given in Freud and Oppenheim's paper on 'Dreams in Folklore' (1957 [1911]), *Standard Ed.*, 12, 187 ff.]

11. [A term vulgarly used for a wealthy spendthrift.]

12. Cf. Jeremias (1904, 115 n.) and Babylonisches im Alten Testament (1906, 96). "'Mamon' ('Mammon') is 'Manman' in Babylonian and is another name for Nergal, the God of the Underworld. According to Oriental mythology, which has passed over into popular legends and fairy tales, gold is the excrement of Hell."

13. [For the occurrence of this in dreams, see a passage added in 1909 to *The Interpretation of Dreams, Standard Ed.*, *4*, 407.]

14. [In English in the original.]

15. [The connection between urethral erotism and ambition seems to find its first mention here. Freud occasionally returned to the point, e.g. in a sentence added in 1914 to *The Interpretation of Dreams, Standard Ed.*, *4*, 216 and in a footnote added in 1920 to the *Three Essays* (1905d), *Standard Ed.*, *7*, 239. In a long footnote to Section III of *Civilization and its Discontents* (1930a) he brought the present finding into connection with his two other main lines of thought concerning enuresis – its symbolic association with fire and its importance as an infantile equivalent of masturbation. See also the still later paper on "The acquisition and control of fire" (1932a).]

16. [There are not many accounts by Freud of the nature of "character" and the mechanism of its formation. Among them may be mentioned a passage near the end of the *Three Essays* (1905d), *Standard Ed.*, *7*, 238–239, some remarks in the paper on "The disposition to obsessional neurosis" (1913), *Standard Ed.*, *12*, 323–324, and especially a discussion in the first half of Chapter III of *The Ego and the Id* (1923b), the gist of which is repeated in Lecture XXXII of the *New Introductory Lectures* (1933a).]

Freud (1917): On transformations of instinct as exemplified in anal erotism*

Some years ago, observations made during psycho-analysis led me to suspect that the constant co-existence in any one of the three character-traits of *orderliness, parsimony* and *obstinacy* indicated an intensification of the anal–erotic components in his sexual constitution, and that these modes of reaction, which were favoured by his ego, had been established during the course of his development through the assimilation of his anal erotism.[1]

In that publication my main object was to make known the fact of this established relation; I was little concerned about its theoretical significance. Since then there has been a general consensus of opinion that each one of the three qualities, avarice, pedantry and obstinacy, springs from anal–erotic sources – or, to express it more cautiously and more completely – draws powerful contributions from those sources. The cases in which these defects of character were combined and which in consequence bore a special stamp (the "anal character") were merely extreme instances, which were bound to betray the particular connection that interests us here even to an unobservant eye.

---

* Freud, S. (1917). On transformations of instinct as exemplified in anal erotism *S.E., 17.*

As a result of numerous impressions, and in particular of one specially cogent analytical observation, I came to the conclusion a few years later that in the development of the libido in man the phase of genital primacy must be preceded by a "pregenital organization" in which sadism and anal erotism play the leading parts.[2]

From that moment we had to face the problem of the later history of the anal–erotic instinctual impulses. What becomes of them when, owing to the establishment of a definitive genital organisation, they have lost their importance in sexual life? Do they preserve their original nature, but in a state of repression? Are they sublimated or assimilated by transformation into character-traits? Or do they find a place within the new organization of sexuality characterized by genital primacy? Or, since none of these vicissitudes of anal erotism is likely to be the only one, to what extent and in what way does each of them share in deciding its fate? For the organic sources of anal erotism cannot of course be buried as a result of the emergence of the genital organization.

One would think that there could be no lack of material from which to provide an answer, since the processes of development and transformation in question must have taken place in everyone undergoing analysis. Yet the material is so obscure, the abundance of ever-recurring impressions so confusing, that even now I am unable to solve the problem fully and can do no more than make some contributions to its solution. In making them I need not refrain from mentioning, where the context allows it, other instinctual transformations besides anal-erotic ones. Finally, it scarcely requires to be emphasised that the developmental events here described – just as the others found in psycho-analysis – have been inferred from the regressions into which they had been forced by neurotic processes.

As a starting-point for this discussion we may take the fact that it appears as if in the products of the unconscious – spontaneous ideas, phantasies and symptoms – the concepts faeces (money, gift),[3] baby and penis are ill-distinguished from one another and are easily interchangeable. We realise, of course, that to express oneself in this way is incorrectly to apply to the sphere of the unconscious terms which belong properly to other regions of mental life, and that we have been led astray by the advantages offered by an analogy. To put the matter in a form less open to objection, these elements in the unconscious are often treated as if they were equivalent and could replace one another freely.

This is most easily seen in the relation between "baby" and "penis". It cannot be without significance that in the symbolic language of dreams, as well as of everyday life, both may be replaced by the same symbol; both baby and penis are called a "little one", ["*das Kleine*"].[4] It is a well-known fact that symbolic speech often ignores difference of sex. The "little one", which originally meant the male genital organ, may thus have acquired a secondary application to the female genitals.

If we penetrate deeply enough into the neurosis of a woman, we not infrequently meet with the repressed wish to possess a penis like a man. We call this wish "envy for a penis" and include it in the castration complex. Chance mishaps in the life of such a woman, mishaps which are themselves frequently the result of a very masculine disposition, have re-activated this infantile wish and, through the backward flow of libido, made it the chief vehicle of her neurotic symptoms. In other women we find no evidence of this wish for a penis; it is replaced by the wish for a baby, the frustration of which in real life can lead to the outbreak of a neurosis. It looks as if such women had understood (although this could not possibly have acted as a motive) that nature has given babies to women as a substitute for the penis that has been denied them. With other women, again, we learn that both wishes were present in their childhood and that one replaced the other. At first they had wanted a penis like a man; then at a later, though still childish, stage there appeared instead the wish for a baby. The impression is forced upon us that this variety in our findings is caused by accidental factors during childhood (e.g., the presence or absence of brothers or the birth of a new baby at some favourable time of life), so that the wish for a penis and the wish for a baby would be fundamentally identical.

We can say what the ultimate outcome of the infantile wish for a penis is in women in whom the determinants of a neurosis in later life are absent: it changes into the wish for a *man,* and thus puts up with the man as an appendage to the penis. This transformation, therefore, turns an impulse which is hostile to the female sexual function into one which is favourable to it. Such women are in this way made capable of an erotic life based on the masculine type of object-love, which can exist alongside the feminine one proper, derived from narcissism. We already know[5] that in other cases it is only a baby that makes the transition from narcissistic self-love to object-love possible. So that in this respect too a baby can be represented by the penis.

I have had occasional opportunities of being told women's dreams that had occurred after their first experience of intercourse. They revealed an unmistakable wish in the woman to keep for herself the penis which she had felt. Apart from their libidinal origin, then, these dreams indicated a temporary regression from man to penis as the object of her wish. One would certainly be inclined to trace back the wish for a man in a purely rationalistic way to the wish for a baby, since a woman is bound to understand sooner or later that there can be no baby without the co-operation of a man. It is, however, more likely that the wish for a man arises independently of the wish for a baby, and that when it arises – from understandable motives belonging entirely to ego-psychology – the original wish for a penis becomes attached to it as an unconscious libidinal reinforcement. The importance of the process described lies in the fact that a part of the young woman's narcissistic masculinity is thus changed into femininity, and so can no longer operate in a way harmful to the female sexual function.

Along another path, a part of the erotism of the pregenital phase, too, becomes available for use in the phase of genital primacy. The baby is regarded as "lumf"[6] (cf. the analysis of "Little Hans"), as something which becomes detached from the body by passing through the bowel. A certain amount of libidinal cathexis which originally attached to the contents of the bowel can thus be extended to the baby born through it. Linguistic evidence of this identity of baby and faeces is contained in the expression "to give someone a baby". For its faeces are the infant's first gift, a part of his body which he will give up only on persuasion by someone he loves, to whom indeed, he will make a spontaneous gift of it as a token of affection; for, as a rule, infants do not dirty strangers. (There are similar if less intense reactions with urine.) Defecation affords the first occasion on which the child must decide between a narcissistic and an object-loving attitude. He either parts obediently with his faeces, "sacrifices" them to his love, or else retains them for purposes of auto-erotic satisfaction and later as a means of asserting his own will. If he makes the latter choice we are in the presence of defiance (obstinacy) which, accordingly, springs from a narcissistic clinging to anal erotism.

It is probable that the first meaning which a child's interest in faeces develops is that of "gift" rather than "gold" or "money". The child knows no money apart from what is given him – no money acquired and none inherited of his own. Since his faeces are his first gift, the child easily transfers his interest from that substance to the new one which he comes across as the most valuable gift in life. Those who question this derivation of gifts should consider their experience of psycho-analytic treatment, study the gifts they receive as doctors from their patients, and watch the storms of transference which a gift from them can rouse in their patients.

Thus the interest in faeces is continued partly as interest in money, partly as a wish for a baby, in which latter an anal–erotic and a genital impulse ("envy for a penis") converge. But the penis has another anal–erotic significance apart from its relation to the interest in a baby. The relationship between the penis and the passage lined with mucous membrane which it fills and excites already has its prototype in the pregenital, anal–sadistic phase. The faecal mass, or as one patient called it, the faecal "stick", represents as it were the first penis, and the stimulated mucous membrane of the rectum represents that of the vagina. There are people whose anal erotism remains vigorous and unmodified up to the age preceding puberty (ten to twelve years); we learn from them that during the pregenital phase they had already developed in phantasy and in perverse play an organisation analogous to the genital one, in which penis and vagina were represented by the faecal stick and the rectum. In other people – obsessional neurotics – we can observe the result of a regressive debasement of the genital organisation. This is expressed in the fact that every phantasy origi- nally conceived on the genital level is transposed to the anal level – the penis being replaced by the faecal mass and the vagina by the rectum.

As the interest in faeces recedes in a normal way, the organic anal- ogy we have described here has the effect of transferring the interest on to the penis. When, later, in the course of the child's sexual researches[7] he discovers that babies are born from the bowel, they inherit the greater part of his anal erotism; they have, however, been preceded by the penis in this as well as in another sense.

I feel sure that by this time the manifold interrelations of the series – faeces, penis, baby – have become totally unintelligible; so I will try to remedy the defect by presenting them diagrammatically [Freud's Figure 2], and in considering the diagram we can review the same material in a different order. Unfortunately, this technical device is not sufficiently pliable for our purpose, or possibly we have not yet learned to use it with effect. In any case I hope the reader will not expect too much from it.

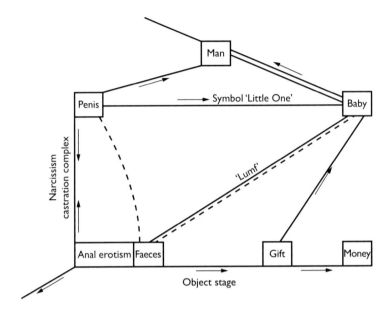

Freud's Figure 2.

Anal erotism finds a narcissistic application in the production of defiance, which constitutes an important reaction on the part of the ego against demands made by other people. Interest in faeces is carried over first to interest in gifts, and then to interest in money. In girls, the discovery of the penis gives rise to envy for it, which later changes into the wish for a man as the possessor of a penis. Even before this the wish for a penis has changed into the wish for a baby, or the latter wish has taken the place of the former one. An organic analogy between penis and baby (dotted line) is expressed by the existence of a symbol ("little one") common to both. A rational wish (double line) then leads from the wish for a baby to the wish for a man: we have already appreciated the importance of this instinctual transformation.

Another part of the nexus of relations can be observed much more clearly in the male. It arises when the boy's sexual researches lead him to the discovery of the absence of a penis in women. He concludes that the penis must be a detachable part of the body, something analogous to faeces, the first piece of bodily substance the child had to part with. Thus the old anal defiance enters into the composition of the castration complex. The organic analogy which enabled the intestinal con-

tents to be the forerunner of the penis during the pregenital phase
cannot come into account as a motive; but the boy's sexual researches
lead him to a psychical substitute for it. When a baby appears on the
scene he regards it as "lumf", in accordance with those researches, and
he cathects it with powerful anal–erotic interest. When social experiences teach that a baby is to be regarded as a love-token, a gift, the
wish for a baby receives a second contribution from the same source.
Faeces, penis and baby are all three solid bodies; they all three, by
forcible entry or expulsion, stimulate a membranous passage, i.e. the
rectum and the vagina, the latter being as it were 'taken on lease' from
the rectum, as Lou Andreas-Salomé aptly remarks.[8] Infantile sexual
researches can only lead to the conclusion that the baby follows the
same route as the faecal mass. The function of the penis is not usually
discovered by those researches. But it is interesting to note that after
so many détours an organic correspondence reappears in the psychical sphere as an unconscious identity.

Notes

1. "Character and Anal Erotism" (1908b).
2. "The [Pre]Disposition to Obsessional Neurosis" (1913i).
3. [The relations between faeces and money, or gold, are discussed at some
    length in the paper already referred to (Freud, 1908b).]
4. [A dream illustrating this will be found in *The Interpretation of Dreams*
    (1900a), *Standard Ed.*, 4, 362 f.]
5. [See the later part of Section II of Freud's paper on narcissism (1914c).]
6. ["Little Hans's" word for faeces. Cf. *Standard Ed.*, 10, 54 and 68n.]
7. [See Freud's paper "On the Sexual Theories of Children" (1908c).]
8. In her paper "'Anal' und 'Sexual'" (1916). [Freud added a footnote in
    1920 to the second of his *Three Essays on Sexuality* (1905, *Standard Ed.*, 7,
    187n.), in which he summarised the contents of that paper.]

References

Andreas-Salomé, L. (1916). "Anal" und "Sexual". *Imago*, 4: 249.
Freud, S. (1900a). *The Interpretation of Dreams*. S.E., 4. London: Hogarth.
Freud, S. (1905d). *Three Essays on the Theory of Sexuality*. S.E., 7: 125–245
    London: Hogarth.

Freud, S. (1908b). On the sexual theories of children. *S.E.*, *9*: 207–226. London: Hogarth.

Freud, S. (1909). *Analysis of a Phobia of a Five-year-old Boy. S.E.*, *10*: 3–149. London: Hogarth.

Freud, S. (1913). The disposition to obsessional neurosis. *S.E.*, *12*: 317–326. London: Hogarth.

Freud, S. (1914). On narcissism: an introduction. *S.E.*, *14*: 73–102. London: Hogarth.

Freud, S. (1923b). *The Ego and the Id. S.E.*, *19*: 3–66. London: Hogarth.

Freud, S. (1923d). A seventeenth-century demonological neurosis. *S.E.*, *19*: 72–108. London: Hogarth.

Freud, S. (1930). *Civilisation and Its Discontents. S.E.*, *21*: 59–145, London: Hogarth.

Freud, S. (1932). The acquisition and control of fire. *S.E.*, *22*: 187–195. London: Hogarth.

Freud, S. (1933). *New Introductory Lectures in Psycho-analysis. S.E.*, *22*. London: Hogarth.

Freud, S. (1950). *Aus den Anfängen der Psychoanalyse*, London.

Freud, S., & Oppenheim, D. E. (1957). *Dreams in Folklore*. New York.

Jeremias, A. (1904). *Das alte Testament im Lichte des alten Orients*. Leipzig.

CHAPTER THREE

Money and childhood phantasies

James Rose and Anca Carrington

O ne of the main proposals of this book is that, because money permits a move from barter to the possibility of separating buying from selling, it enables three people to be involved in financial activity. Thus, someone can buy something from a supplier and sell it on to a third party. This separation enables a much greater complexity in social and economic structure. It permits a specialisation of production, buying and selling activity, enabling an avoidance of duplication of effort. A currency (in the form of money) mediating these exchanges to take place conveniently could be said, thus, to make society possible and allow advance from tribal communities to a nation state. A consequence of this advance is that it inevitably creates a different social setting that leads to considerable diversification of feelings to be contained by the social structure and the organisations and institutions created to manage them. As Chapter Four shows, these institutions are not always best equipped to recognise and address the emotional undercurrent associated with financial transactions, with consequences that reach beyond their immediate remit. This transmission mechanism reflects something about the self-similar structure of monetary exchanges, where deeply rooted emotional tensions are combined and replicated in similar ways at various levels of functioning—individuals, corporations, markets, and society. This recurring relationship is evocative of fractals, that is to say, of structures where the same pattern can be identified at different scales of measurement—as they appear in snowflakes or tree branches, for example. Their strength in nature is that they provide maximum surface and, therefore, optimise contact with the environment (Barrow, 2005), something that is also relevant to the human emotional experience.

In broad terms, we might say that the emotional experience of individuals in the barter-based society will be typified by those of a two-person situation and, thereby, potentially paranoid, following the formulations of Klein (1946), even though the exchange is clearly public to the two parties. Thus, even though the bartering pair can both see and experience the nature of the exchange in an overt way, there is still room for many fantasies about the other person and the quality of the goods exchanged. There can, therefore, be intense feelings evoked by this situation with no third party to mediate in the transaction. When money is the currency of economic exchange, we might expect that the resulting three-person situation expands the spectrum of emotional possibilities. When one of the triad is absent in any one economic transaction, this absence creates the opportunity to stimulate intense feelings, which can be hard for individuals or institutions to contain. This phantasy might take the form of the participants wondering who has got the best deal, thereby evoking jealousy and envy. This can then give rise to a strong feeling that someone is being exploited. The intensity of feeling that might result in certain situations will mean that calm and rational decision making and debate becomes difficult to maintain, no matter how desirable this might be. In an atmosphere of competition or economic depression, this will be likely to be exacerbated.

If we then ask what forms of feelings might emerge, it seems likely that they might be expected to be similar to those aroused in any situation of anxiety. The greater the anxiety, the more powerful will these feelings be, making clear thinking and rational analysis increasingly difficult. A psychoanalytic perspective on this would suggest that, if we are to understand what happens as anxiety increases and the resulting feelings become more powerful, we may learn a great deal from the study of the development of the emotional life of children. In essence, as they grow to maturity, they will experience these feelings and, with the help of their parents, learn to manage them and, indeed, to use them creatively. There is nothing abnormal and pathological implied by this approach. However, it does imply a process of emotional learning and growth through which every person must progress and each will experience this learning in their own idiosyncratic way.

Emotional learning and development is clearly a very big subject, the understanding of which has stimulated an enormous literature, and it is beyond the scope of this book to provide a full summary of it. Furthermore, while it might be useful to have a behavioural description of these processes, it seems more helpful here to try to get as close as is possible to describing the experience of these feelings.

There is surprisingly little literature covering the relationship children have with money. One possible explanation is that childhood phantasies are the precursor of later relationship patterns and that, while their shape is generic in the early years, the link with money only becomes established and fashioned by them once dealing with actual currency in the external reality. This provides access to the versatile vehicle of emotional currency of internal reality transactions. Another explanation might be that much of the child analysis literature focuses on early pathology, and the struggles children have with relating to their internal and external objects, of which money does not become explicitly one until later in life.

One illuminating exception that links Freud's 1905 insights into infantile sexuality, or the impact of the drives on childhood everyday life, away from pathology, but on the pliable boundary between internal and external specific to that age, is the concluding chapter of Davidson and Fay's (1952) *Phantasy in Childhood*, titled "The living-through of phantasies". What is noteworthy about this contribution is its emphasis on ordinary development and the focus on the forceful, engaging presence that phantasies play in it. Phantasy, as opposed to fantasy, as it is ordinarily spelt, is used here to emphasise that these are often unconscious and, possibly, all the more forceful as a result. This follows Klein's analysis of unconscious phantasy, or the unconscious psychic representation of the drives identified by Freud. Also, in the particular example described by Davidson and Fay, the issue of money is present in the background, defining the modest material circumstances of this family's life. The quality of the attention to the moment-by-moment changes in the state of mind and responses of the memorable little girl, Dinah, who is the focus of this chapter, has very much the subtle and nuanced tone of infant observation literature (e.g., Miller et al., 2002).

Davidson and Fay seek to illustrate how phantasies work constantly at shaping our understanding of reality, while being shaped in turn by changes in the external world. In childhood, each of these changes—weaning, moving house, birth of a sibling—is full of emotional impact, as the frontier between the internal and external worlds is particularly permeable and changes occur with a degree of urgency. It is not possible to know at which subsequent point this process slows down, but one could argue that, in ordinary life, the boundary is never quite saturated and the weaving process of inner and outer reality continues. In terms of pathology, it is conceivable that problems arise when either saturation occurs, so that the exchange between the internal and external worlds becomes blocked, or when the permeability is so high that no structure or separation is possible.

While we cannot reproduce here the long and detailed description by Davidson and Fay *in toto*, it is possible to identify and explore certain themes which all must negotiate in their growth to maturity. Acknowledging that this exploration will only address part of the overall picture, these themes will give a taste of the developmental tasks and the feelings evoked in their negotiation. They form a part of the process through which the individual learns to distinguish their internal world from the realities of the external world. The individual can be only partly conscious of this internal world of which much remains undiscovered—or unconscious. Moreover, each individual achieves this in their idiosyncratic way and their resulting internal world provides the matrix framing the individual's experience of anything that stirs strong feelings, that is to say, the template for managing and experiencing their emotional currency and, thus, their lives. Money has the potential to stir strong feelings because, in certain situations, it is the currency of transaction between people, in both the emotional and financial sense. The themes listed below all have the potential to evoke strong feelings, each of them with an open valency towards the corresponding emotional impact of money. These include *inter alia*: dependency, personal value of oneself and one's contents, possessions, rivalry and competition, all present and vibrantly consequential from early life. When money becomes part of the currency of these situations, it becomes associated inevitably with these strong feelings. These associations will not be experienced in an identical manner by all but we can see that these situations will be experienced emotionally in some way by everyone. Any parents, like any witness of protracted pay negotiations, will see these themes informing the meaning of the situation to the parties concerned in the negotiations.

The emotional themes that will be considered are:

1. The experience of dependency.
2. The discovery of likes and dislikes.
3. The discovery of personal contents—physical and psychological.
4. The discovery of relationships both with another individual and within an oedipal triangle.

The experience of dependency

The human infant begins life in a state of dependency upon his parents. It is, of course, a total dependency, and this is crucial to survival. The importance of the patterns of attachment that an infant establishes with her mother has been the subject of considerable study (e.g., Bowlby, 1979) as has their consequence for a child's experience and later life. Davidson and Fay describe the behaviour of Dinah feeding from her mother's breast in the first weeks of life thus: "From the beginning she had a voracious appetite and would suck passionately, gulping down so much milk that she often vomited, and continuing to suck until the breast was emptied" (p. 140). As adult observers, we might infer that the baby is, and feels, engaged in a struggle for survival. We cannot say what her conscious experience actually is, but the energy and passion of what we see will probably suggest to us a struggle for survival, if she is deprived of what she needs. As the availability of money can be crucial to survival, we can see that its threatened absence has the potential to evoke the kinds of feelings we infer from witnessing a feeding baby. In maturity in later life, when we have established an ongoing economic security, we are unlikely to experience the same kind of panic. However, we can infer that the absence of money, because it signifies survival, always has the potential to evoke this panic. Threats, arising from dependency, will inevitably become part of the meaning of money because of what its lack will signify. The increase in suicide rates associated with rises in unemployment and incidences of financial crashes testify to the widespread nature of the fear that life cannot be sustained in the presence of sudden financial losses, where the absence of money turns from phantasy to reality and, thus, threatens, and sometimes brings total annihilation of, the individual.

Dependency is often experienced in the context of deprivation, and money can function as the means to bypass the discomfort this evokes. Dinah remarks on something lacking in everything around her, including "Water got no hands" (Davidson & Fay, 1952, p. 150), and wishes her mother to buy teeth or a nose for her dolly. Equally, a sense of deprivation becomes combined with a wish to repair the damage perceived, money serving well in this task, even for a child:

> . . . alongside Dinah's sense of having been attacked and deprived by her mother, there was a feeling that the mother herself was injured. One day she remarked, on inspecting the washing: 'Mummy's knick-knicks broken; must buy another one in a shop'—although they were really intact. (p. 152)

In adult life, the phantasy of effecting reparation by spending money is easily and often acted out, but by individuals and at the level of society. The exit out of crisis and the damage it has inflicted upon the economy and the people within it is often portrayed as accessible by increasing spending, by individuals, companies, and governments alike.

The discovery of likes and dislikes

As a child develops and their diet diversifies, once weaning has been achieved, we can observe a child experiencing some new food and reacting with pleasure or distaste. Some foods they enjoy taking in and other foods are rejected. Davidson and Fay observe this about Dinah:

> Apart from this one period, and times when she completely rejected vegetables, her feeding was satisfactory, with great enjoyment of milk, eggs, and cheese, and normal likes and dislikes which were permitted without any forcing. Throughout, eating was a source of pleasure, and she had a positive relationship with her food, which . . . included the wish to ensure that the food she ate enjoyed being inside her. (pp. 141–142)

We see here a child learning both to regulate what they take in and to relate to it. This is the beginning of the establishment of body boundaries, with the implied sense of what is inside the body and what is kept outside. Quite what it is that determines these preferences for any one individual is hard to say, but the important point here is the establishment of a sense of inner and outer which lays the foundation for the experience of bodily contents. Davidson and Fay mention the importance of this to the child they observed, with Dinah wishing to ensure that she felt that the food she ate enjoyed being inside her, suggesting a very different attitude to food from that which adults might experience.

We can imagine that her experience illustrates the establishing of the foundations needed for recognising and managing change: from breastfeeding to new food—indeed, from one new food to many. Money is intrinsically linked with (ex-)change, as we often speak of receiving any change or not from many daily transactions. Although we do not think of capital Change when receiving a few small coins when we buy a book, for instance, money and change have travelled together for a long time, so that the link between the two is a well-established one in our minds. We talk of "small change" and "no change", but perhaps less and less so as electronic exchanges make many such transactions once removed and, thus, more indirect. Change is, thus, also once removed in its mechanisms, but nevertheless present in its consequences, as the recent financial crises have shown.

The discovery of personal contents: physical and psychological implications

Defecation provides the child with the experience of something coming, or being produced, from within them. Davidson and Fay describe how Dinah reacted to this experience. During the first few months, the act of defecation often appeared to be painful to her, although her motions were quite loose; by four months, however, there were times when this obviously gave her pleasure, as for example, on one occasion, after the insertion of a suppository. Between the ages of eleven months and one year, she occasionally smeared her faeces, doing so quietly while she was in her play-pen and evidently enjoying it.

> When she was about a year, her mother began now and again to intro-
> duce the pot, but did not insist when each time it was refused. At 1.1
> Dinah would sometimes lift her skirt with a slightly guilty air after
> wetting on the floor, and on seeing a puddle would exclaim: 'Oh God,
> wee-wee!'—even if, as on one occasion, it was only some spilt beer!
> When she was 1.3 and was going through an extremely positive and
> affectionate phase in regard to her mother, she would sit on the pot
> willingly, with an air of great pride and satisfaction, and would listen
> to the tinkle of urine with delight, chuckling. She would gaze at her
> mother with a loving smile when urinating and defaecating, and on
> some occasions clung to her and passionately pressed her face against
> hers. During this period she was sometimes reluctant to get off the pot,
> and liked to inspect and touch its contents, although she would not
> stay on it at all if left alone. (Davidson & Fay, 1952, p. 142)

To adult eyes, it might be intriguing, not to say a source of amusement or irritation, to observe a child enjoying their faeces—for
instance, smearing—without any sense of adult disgust. But, we can
see from the above narrative, that defecation becomes part of the
emotional interplay between this child and her mother, upon whom
she depends. The pleasure that her mother communicates to her
daughter becomes part of the emotional currency of affection between
the two. For the child, producing her contents for mother is as pleas-
ing as it may be for her mother as toilet training sucessfully pro-
gresses. It becomes a kind of co-celebration of the child's contents and,
at some level, the child herself.

In the early years of life, the child's experience of good things
coming into them (because of their pleasure) and good things coming
out of them (because of mother's pleasure) seems to set the stage for
a satisfactory differentiation between inner and outer and the existence of an effective boundary separating them.

Hayman (1974) offers an interesting study of what she calls anal
phantasies. In particular, she describes a little boy who, in early life,
suffered a serious scalding necessitating hospitalisation. This painful
experience seemed to lead to a reluctance to go to the toilet because
the faeces were experienced as burning, a link with the painful scalding. However, this was not the whole story.

In his analysis, the little boy

> ... soon declared his disbelief in jobbies really vanishing down the
> lavatory, thus expressing, among other things, his great wish not to

lose them, a wish that was connected with his identifying jobbies with babies. After a few months in analysis he verbalized his wish to bear a baby. During the second half of his first year in analysis he often led with increasing knowledge into the matter of how males and females differ anatomically. When he really knew, intellectually, that only males have a "penis = weewee", and only females have a "baby hole" and can bear babies, he increasingly became able to express his contrary wish by saying determinedly or wistfully that "*Some* boys, *some* men can have babies." (Hayman, 1974, p. 270)

We can see the positive evaluation of faeces through the equation with babies. We also see the interweaving of his experience of defecation with his understanding of his body and of those of men and women.

We can also see the basis for Freud's suggestion of the association between faeces and money because of their association with owning, creating, and giving. In contrast with adult disgust, faeces are valuable to the child because they represent something that comes from within them (and that they, therefore, create), which they then give, as a gift, to mother, to her obvious pleasure. We can imagine the consequences for the child if their creations are treated with disgust.

Beyond the relationship between this and giving and receiving gifts in adult life, the early experience of contents also provides a template for dealing with loss. Commerce and the early uses of money related to the simple transactions of buying and selling: the former, a way of denying deprivation and loss, a way of making good anything desired but missing, the latter a relieving of that fundamental experience of having one's offerings valued and rewarded, time and again, as compensation for the loss entailed.

The discovery of relationships both with another individual and within an oedipal triangle

The triangle here is described as oedipal in deference to Freud, who used the Greek myth of Oedipus to describe the situation in which children found themselves in relation to their parents as they approached the end of the time in their lives preceding the arrival of puberty. In other words, the child experienced him/herself as part of a triangle in a new way.

The growing awareness of conscious enjoyment that the child experiences in her relationship with mother sets the scene for further development. Mother, of course, will not always be satisfying her child's needs. Indeed, sometimes she will have to frustrate them, and this will create an emotional reaction in the child of distress, protest, and anger. We can infer, therefore, that Mother is, in the child's experience, sometimes good and sometimes bad. Into this scene of the mother–child pair will step a third party, possibly to be turned to at times of the child's distress and frustration. At the same time, this third might be the presumed cause of mother's absence and of her turning away, and, in that sense, a rival for her attention, someone who engages mother in another pairing, from which the child finds herself excluded. The world in which the child lives becomes instantly more complex. A whole new spectrum of feelings becomes possible, as the parents/adults might identify these feelings and name them.

Side by side with this will come, as a result of the child's discovery of their own insides, a sense that mother, too, has an inside. Davidson and Fay (1952) give a graphic example of how little Dinah started to become aware of her mother's insides:

> When Dinah was 2.6, the family had a chicken for lunch which had eggs in it, and explanations were given to her older cousins. Dinah herself did not seem interested at the time, but a few days later, at bedtime, she asked: 'Have you got eggs in your tummy like a chicken, Mummy?' Her mother replied 'No', feeling later that her answer had been terse and inadequate. (pp. 160–161)

One might feel that little Dinah, for all her apparent disinterest, was, in fact, listening very closely and was intensely curious. Somehow, perhaps, she was sensitive to her mother's reticence at the time, but the question she asked later reveals her curiosity and memory of the event. Before this incident, Dinah is reported as becoming interested in the differences between her own body and that of a male cousin, which was noticed when they were bathed together. She remarks on their "tailies" and her lack of one. Davidson and Fay report that "Three weeks later, inspecting her genitals while sitting on the pot, she remarked with a humorous expression: 'I got no taily', and at another time: 'Mummy got no taily. Daddy got one, and Jim, too'" (p. 159).

There is, through these incidents, evidence of the stirring of a curiosity about where babies come from and how they get there in the first place. This reaches a kind of *dénoument* with the arrival on the

scene of her younger brother, when Dinah reveals her growing awareness thus:

One day she spontaneously remarked: "Mans can't have babies."
Later she said: "What does Jim have a tail for?" Her mother replied:
"So as to be a daddy when he grows up", and Dinah said: "Jim has a
tiny weeny taily, and when he grows up he will have a huge enormous taily like his daddy Peter and my daddy Ben, and then everybody will have two daddies." One day, while examining herself in the
bath, the following conversation took place:

Dinah: "Little boys have got tailies there, but I haven't. What have I
got?"

Mother: "A little hole."

Dinah: "And what goes into that hole?"

Mother: "Nothing just now."

Another day, also examining her genitals:

Dinah: "What's that called?"

Mother: "It's a little hole."

Dinah: "Who lives in that hole?"

Mother: "Nobody."

Dinah: "That's a pretend house and pretend people live in it. What's it
called? What does Daddy call it?"

Mother: "What would you like to call it?"

Dinah: "Noot, because only pretend people live in it."

Mother: "What sort of people?"

Dinah: "Pretend baby people. Is it a taily?"

Mother: "No."

Dinah: "What does Daddy have a taily for?"

Mother: "All daddies have tailies."

In these conversations Dinah clearly showed that she very well knew
the functions of the penis and vagina, although she had never been
told. (pp. 161–162)

In seeing and reading about these events, we, with our adult minds, may well infer that Dinah is becoming conscious of living with a mother and a father, who have brought her into the world. Furthermore, the knowledge of the different functions of penises and vaginas (or, in her understanding, tailies and holes) could be thought of as evidence of showing her constant curiosity and her taking in far more, albeit in her own way of understanding, than we adults, or her parents, might have imagined. With awareness of what parents can do (i.e., bring their siblings into the world), and how they do it, and of how mummies and daddies are sometimes lovely and sometimes naughty, as they gratify or frustrate their child, we can see the impact of living this triangular situation to a child.

Their parents can seem powerful (creating strong feeling and a sense of vulnerability), fascinating (provoking intense curiosity, having a life of their own not known to the baby), become sources of feelings of a drive for their affection and competition with siblings, and are seen as being in possession of knowledge not immediately available to, and possibly withheld from, the child.

While we look at this situation through adult eyes and experience it with our adult bodies, we cannot avoid our own memories of these events in our own lives. We may infer that any situation that approximates to this triangular situation, and which provokes much anxiety, will inevitably evoke similar strong feelings. We might hypothesise that money, because of its essentially triangulating property, will unavoidably create situations which will evoke strong feelings and anxieties about survival and destruction.

The themes that we have explored in this description of a little girl's development will be readily seen by the reader as being very basic to her experience and to our own. The themes of dependency (and helplessness), likes and dislikes (involving pleasure and fear), personal contents (with the connotations of possessions and identity), and the discovery of parents and siblings (with the connotations of belonging and rivalry) will strike a strong resonance with everyone's emotional life. This is quite normal and inescapable. The experience of money—because it is a crucial part of exchange between people—will, therefore, inevitably have the potential to stir up all these feelings and, thereby, symbolise and signify them. The impact of these feelings will affect economic decision making, with potentially disastrous effects, as we shall see in the next chapter. This is followed by explorations of what money can come to symbolise and signify to those involved in financial transactions, no matter how large or small: in other words, all of us. It may be concluded that we cannot afford to turn a blind eye to the impact that we make through money and allow money to have upon our lives.

References

Barrow, J. D. (2005). *The Artful Universe Expanded*. Oxford: Oxford University Press.

Bowlby, J. (1979). *The Making and Breaking of Affectional Bonds*. London: Tavistock [reprinted Routledge, 2005].

Davidson, A., & Fay, J. (1952). *Phantasy in Childhood*. London: Routledge & Kegan Paul [reprinted Westport, CT: Greenwood Press, 1972].

Hayman, A. (1974). Some unusual anal fantasies of a young child. *Psychoanalytic Study of the Child*, 29: 265–276.

Klein, M. (1946). Some notes on schizoid mechanisms. *International Journal of Psychoanalysis*, 27: 99–110.

Miller, L., Rustin, M., Rustin, M., & Shuttleworth, J. (2002). *Closely Observed Infants*. Eastbourne: Duckworth.

CHAPTER FOUR

Phantasy in the world economy

Anca Carrington

Introduction

E stablished with great subtlety and strength in our early years, phantasies remain a much relied upon solution to navigating the emotional journey that our daily experiences set us upon throughout life.

It is particular to psychoanalysis that it can offer insight into how the forces of unconscious phantasy, psychic reality, and changing states of mind enter into every human decision or interaction, including those we are often inclined to attribute to experts, or those that we habitually regard as unavoidable collective outcomes.

As an illustration of the impact of phantasy in relationship to money beyond childhood, this chapter offers a novel take on financial markets, through a seminal contribution in the application of the standard frame of psychoanalytic understanding of human psychology in the realm of economic life. The paper reproduced here, initially published in 2008, constituted a stepping stone towards fresh insight into the human factor in the economic domain, developed in unprecedented subtlety of detail by Tuckett (2011), and continues to inspire efforts to reorientate economic thinking towards a more integrated recognition of the impact of uncertainty in terms of emotional conflicts and their implications for market participants and society.

Central to the argument by Tuckett and Taffler (2008) is the link between the role of narrative in supporting human perception and action, by organising facts and feelings in the presence of uncertainty, and the role of phantasy as a template for narratives that matter to us and help to orientate us emotionally. From their deep and strong childhood roots, phantasies continue to dominate our internal lives, often with consequences that stretch far beyond the individual experience. The authors show how the stream of technical expertise and rational thinking of agents in the financial markets is constantly shaped and often undermined by an emotional undercurrent which stems not from pathology, but from ordinary development, of the kind brought to life by the illustration in Chapter Three. Building on the psychoanalytic understanding of how reality is experienced in different states of mind, and of the role of phantasy in navigating the perpetual tension between the reality principle and the pleasure principle, the authors analyse the role of attitudes of mind and emotional responses to shaping outcomes in the financial markets. In particular, they expand on the role of phantastic objects, that is, of mental representations of entities invested with the power to do away with the tension between reality and pleasure, in delivering the promise of satisfying desire and eliminating all emotional barriers to it, in a way that we have seen is linked intrinsically to money.

As we have seen in Chapter Three, the fundamental challenges of uncertainty and ambivalence are present and demand to be confronted from the beginning of life. Specifically, as Klein (1935) posited, all threatening tensions are avoided from the start by separating and distancing the "good" from the "bad", with the capacity to integrate and tolerate their coexistence being established only gradually, as loss and guilt become bearable. In some sense, this integration is never fully achieved, as indicated by the universal fascination with stories where good and bad confront and battle each other time and again. Rather then seeing splitting and integration as developmental stages, Britton (1998) proposed that the two extremes are states of mind between which we oscillate throughout life, day to day and even moment to moment.

The names of these states or positions in the psychoanalytic literature (paranoid-schizoid (PS) or depressive (D)) evoke pathology and unease, yet the experiences they refer to are universal and ordinary in the development of the human psyche. Also, it is not just individuals who can find themselves in these states, but also groups, which can oscillate between sustaining a capacity to experience reality and attend to the shared task, with some degree of anxiety (known as work group), and the pure pursuit of omnipotent and omniscient phantasy satisfaction (basic assumption group) that banishes anxiety and gives rein to wishful thinking (see Bott Spillius et al., 2011, pp. 259–261 for further details on these group states). In such scenarios, the individual capacity to accept or avoid reality is either reinforced or overridden by the urge to belong to the group. Teams, companies, and professions all share the qualities of a group.

Finally, the importance of path dependency explored here is twofold, as it helps understand changes in the financial markets in their historical context, as much as it illuminates the continuity in the workings of the mind and the traceable links of adult emotional experiences to their very early and powerful roots.

The original 2008 paper by Tuckett and Taffler is preceded here by a new introduction by David Tuckett, providing an update on recent developments in understanding the fast changing and consequential world of the financial markets.

References

Bott Spillius, E., Milton, J., Garvey, P., Couve, C., & Steiner, D. (2011). *The New Dictionary of Kleinian Thought*. London: Routledge.

Britton, R. S. (1998). Before and after the depressive position Ps(n)->D(n) ->Ps(n+1). In: *Belief and Imagination: Explorations in Psychoanalysis* (pp. 69–81). London: Routledge.

Klein, M. (1935). A contribution to the psychogenesis of manic–depressive states. *International Journal of Psychoanalysis*, 16: 145–174.

Tuckett, D. (2011). *Minding the Markets: An Emotional Finance View of Financial Instability*. Basingstoke: Palgrave Macmillan.

Tuckett, D., & Taffler, T. (2008). Phantastic objects and the financial market's sense of reality: A psychoanalytic contribution to the understanding of stock market instability, *International Journal of Psychoanalysis, 89*: 389–412.

Overview and introduction by David Tuckett

T his paper, first published in early 2008, marked a formal attempt to set out for peer review by the psychoanalytic community a theory of financial instability. It had begun with observations that Richard Taffler and I made during and after the dot com bubble, which had been worked out and presented in various financial or university settings (Tuckett & Taffler, 2003), some of which were published in a *Financial Times* article just prior to the collapse of Northern Rock (Taffler & Tuckett, 2007). The paper was drafted between 2004 and 2007 before completing an interview study of fund managers (Tuckett, 2011; Tuckett & Taffler, 2012) and finalised in the summer of 2007 just as credit markets first froze in August and the global financial crisis was about to break.

The central idea is that the financial bubble trajectories to which financial markets are subject exhibit a path-dependent sequence of self-reinforcing unconscious phantasy narratives and emotional states. Self-reinforcing feedback and feed-forward processes occur at emotional, cognitive, and technical (i.e., Ponzi process) levels. What happens is that the institutionally supported tendency to pursue what we termed "phantastic objects" in normal times occasionally captures the market, spreading beyond the financial community to society at large, and takes over in such way that the market's sense of reality is seriously compromised. Phantastic objects stimulate what Bion described as a PS (paranoid-schizoid) state of mind, a process further enabled by basic assumption group processes. These ideas have proved useful and remain at the core of theories I have subsequently developed. However, partly to avoid confusion or the creation of any impression that we intended to psychologise or pathologise market participants, I have subsequently adopted the term *divided* state for PS, *integrated* state for D (depressive), and *groupfeel* for basic assumption group (Tuckett, 2011).

Work since 2008 has focused on seeking to influence both academic and professional discussion of economics and finance. Working with a team comprising psychologists, computer scientists, and social anthropologists, I have conducted additional empirical studies to develop the position set out in 2008, seeking to understand how and why financial markets produce outcomes that fail all but a handful of people—distorting economy and society as well as seriously disturbing trust and social cohesion.

The central idea is that a significant cause of current outcomes is a failure of thought, specifically a denial in economics and the decision sciences of the problems posed by radical or ontological (Lane & Maxfield, 2005) uncertainty. Rather than follow what became the conventional wisdom in economics, that is, to think about financial markets as if they are a reliable means for establishing value forced by competitive pressure to be relatively efficient, we might, rather, try to understand them as they actually are: as contexts ruled by efforts to manage radical uncertainty and the emotional conflicts this necessarily creates. The position rests on the observations in my interviews, but first made by Keynes (1936) and subsequently largely ignored, that commitments to act with consequences for the long term cannot be modelled on calculation alone.

Radical uncertainty and the production of emotion

Consider the nature of all financial assets. It is an elementary but sometimes overlooked fact that they are very different to most other objects bought and sold in exchange, for instance television sets. Fundamentally, this is because although their future values exhibit some patterns and some path dependency, what they are worth is always uncertain and volatile through time. Linked to this, they are abstract derivative entities worth nothing in themselves—valuable because of what they are expected to be worth in future. It depends on imagining, creating a story about, how future cash flows from the underlying entity will be generated in a competitive market and the complex interactions of the views of others about such scenarios. Intrinsic value in this situation is essentially unknowably uncertain—particularly for complex products or companies. Moreover, liquidity can dry up unpredictably if the narrative changes and trust evaporates. The prices of assets can become zero.

If you want a television, you can research price and quality, purchase it, take it home, and watch it. So long as it goes on working you have made your decision and that is it. Not so with financial assets, whether you purchase them and hold them as a professional or client or as a manager or director of an investment bank overseeing an institution valued by what happens to them tomorrow, your decision is never final. It has to be made again and again and again.

Because their future value is volatile and necessarily dependent on a narrative about a future yet to happen, the moment-by-moment price of financial assets is continuously subject to radical uncertainty and its close cousin, information ambiguity. Safe assets by convention at one moment can become risky assets at another, if the narrative changes. In consequence, all forms of asset management necessarily stimulate emotions. There is *excitement about the prospect of gain* when their values are expected to go up and *anxiety about loss* when they are thought to be at risk of going down. In any period, portfolio values of a basket of assets of any sort are likely to go down as much as up—even if the overall trend in a longer period is up. Portfolio management by the most hardened professional, therefore, must always be about managing the feelings this volatility creates for them and their clients.

The economics literature on uncertainty discusses only uncertainty aversion. It misses the fundamental dilemma with which decision makers must contend. Uncertainty certainly creates anxiety about loss and so acts as a dangerous repeller. But it also creates opportunity and is an attractor—causing excitement about potential gain. These are powerful emotions well known to psychoanalysis that automatically stimulate neurotransmitter pathways in the brain's reward system.

Creating financial narratives

Try to visualise anything you plan to do today and in future. What you will be doing is creating a story, linking your aims and objectives to pictures and feelings about ways of fulfilling them, at some level based on unconscious phantasy. Perception works in much the same way. Creating narratives is the human way to recognise patterns and organise thoughts and feeling to create meaning, coherence, and conviction. Narrative conviction lies at the heart of the way human perception works to support action in uncertainty.

Financial narratives also provide scripts to allow investors to act. They attract them to a choice, repel anxiety, and explain and rationalise action. Whether underpinned by complex quantitative calculations, gut feelings, rules of thumb, extensive research processes, or group conversations, what narratives do within the social and institutional context in which they are created is to organise facts and feelings. Once completed, narratives feel right. They allow agents to take, and then to stick to, decisions when (*ex ante*) they cannot know what precisely it was right to do. Everyone at every intermediary level is creating a narrative of the future. It is why financial markets, in which the underlying values of assets in the future are unknowable, are best understood as markets in narratives. Prices reflect consensus narratives about future value and, of course, can change much quicker than the world they seek to describe and explain.

Given this reality, understanding market outcomes depends on asking about the circumstances in which agents as a group manage to feel comfortable enough to act at all in this situation and with what consequences. They must create mental relationships that attach them to the underlying investment objects and continue to do so as time plays out. Uncertain rewards and possible punishments are at stake. So, as in love relations, relationships to financial assets are much like other dependent relations. They necessarily create ambivalence, alternating experiences of loving the object (idealising) and hating (being made uncomfortable by) it.

To do the job, one must be able to become attracted to the object (idea) and stay attracted to it, and to do so must overcome the ever-present potential for doubts and distrust—but not so much that one becomes blind. The problem is that the market reality of price volatility and ambiguous and ever-changing information flows continuously create constant grounds for ambivalence. To maintain even medium term conviction—and even more so the kind of long-term relationship that worthwhile projects in the "real" economy usually require—is an emotional and cognitive challenge.

Phantastic object narratives

The challenge is managed every day by creating what we term "conviction" narratives (Chong & Tuckett, 2013; Tuckett & Nikolic, 2014; Tuckett, Smith, & Nyman, 2014). Conviction narratives are necessary for action and prevent paralysis. But in that context *divided states* can interact with *phantastic object narratives.*

Phantastic object narratives are a special class of narrative—stories about objects of desire, love, idealisation, and excitement that Richard Taffler and I introduced in the paper below. They are stories about how to get great returns for average or low risk: exciting stories about new ways of doing business, new financial products, new ways of managing risk, new technologies, new asset classes, new areas of the world, or new ways of creating loans to sell houses or engage in other activities. The power of phantastic object narratives is that they offer relationships to subjectively very attractive idealised "objects" (people, ideas, or things—tulips, dot coms, derivative options, emerging markets, star analysts and managers). In their psyche, narrators can imagine (feel rather than think) that their deepest desires can yet be satisfied. Narratives support the belief, therefore, that the very unusual is possible. In everyday markets, phantastic object narratives are continuously being created by financial intermediaries and their clients, as exemplified by the deeply entrenched but largely false belief that more than a handful of agents demonstrate the skill to achieve consistent exceptional performance (see Tuckett & Taffler, 2012).

The problem with phantastic objects is that they are not real. We idealise to overcome the problems of uncertainty and ambivalence that otherwise threaten our attachment and so make us insecure. Reality, which is a complex mixture of satisfaction and frustration, *should* modify idealisation and gradually create real experiences of the value of trust. If, however, relationships remain based on idealisation, then reality will be a constant threat.

Relations founded on phantastic object narratives, therefore, are inherently unstable and fragile. They can only be maintained for lengthy periods in what I term *divided states* of mind, simplistic states in which the everyday anxiety-producing ideas thrown up by reality are present in the mind but not consciously experienced and so not available for conscious thinking. *Divided states* are black and white and so can be contrasted with more complex *integrated states* of mind with shades of grey. In these, anxiety is tolerated so that the reasons for doubt and trust can be retained in awareness and become objects for conscious or level-headed thought.

Divided states belong to individuals but are facilitated and supported by what I term *groupfeel*, a state of affairs where a group of people (which can be a virtual group) orientate their thoughts and action to each other based on a powerful and not fully conscious wish not to be different and to feel the same. It leads to black and white groupthink.

Narrative as a focus for cross-disciplinary research

Narratives are used by human actors to organise large quantities of data and create conviction about its interpretation—they combine cognitive and affective elements. In a complex information environment (i.e., where the interpretation of information is uncertain so that how to reach goals is uncertain), conviction narratives enable action and rationalise actions taken, the latter helping to sustain action. They are, therefore, vital parts of decision making, especially under uncertainty where paradigmatic (statistical) methods of establishing truth are not available (see Tuckett, 2012).

Aggregated conviction narratives move society. This is because individual narratives (developed in social groups and other networks) sometimes co-ordinate and converge into shared narratives about future options and policies. They are strongly influenced by group social and psychological effects and inherently fragile and unstable. Whereas the state of the world changes rather slowly, the state of narratives about what is happening in it can alter very sharply and is strongly subject to social interaction and influence. Recent events in financial markets have demonstrated this proposition forcibly, but it also happens in relation to health theories, crime theories, climate change theories, and so on.

We have been using the Reuters news archive to show that very large quantities of text data (over fourteen million stories) can successfully be analysed rigorously using algorithmic methodology to capture shifts in societal and cultural narratives of potentially great subtlety and importance. Because, hitherto, subjective opinions, judgements, accounts, and feelings have been hard to investigate reliably, their obvious importance for many social and political issues has often been underestimated—"numerical" data has been easier to collect and process and decision makers have had to fly blind when assessing opinion, and to communicate blind as well. Now the existence of large online real time text in public and private datasets allows relatively unobtrusive examination of historical shifts in things such as narrative sentiment and the exploration of social and psychological theories (see Tuckett, Smith, & Nyman, 2013).

Incentives and performance evaluation

The dilemmas thrown up by the nature of financial assets just described create a problem for determining incentives and judging performance. At the end of a period, some assets are worth more than others. However, given uncertainty and the characteristics of assets, it is very difficult to separate skill from luck in achieving such outcomes. Confident performance evaluation is difficult. This must be why very few investment mandates are evaluated in a truly long-term way and most evaluations end up being short-term—much shorter than the periods required to evaluate most real-world activities.

In the past few years, we have all been bystanders to claims of fantastic success and then failure in banking and asset management institutions. It illustrates how success in finance can be quite illusory and that, in the end, performance evaluation is really about creating and evaluating narratives. Difficulties arise as some narratives cease to inspire belief.

In sum, the view made possible by the research begun in the paper below is that radical uncertainty and the dilemmas it creates mean that financial markets are very likely to suffer from disturbances of thought derived from capture by phantastic object narratives, divided states, and groupfeel. Such narratives and states can be seen everywhere in the financial world. They are exemplified by a glance at headlines—star traders, star asset managers, and star analysts—and at the literature used to market most financial products. Institutional hiring practices and incentives follow. As organised in this way, financial markets cannot tend to equilibrium and efficiency. Rather, they are the unco-ordinated and uncontrolled producers of instability, inequality, and inefficiency. They need to be approached, theorised, and regulated from this viewpoint.

References

Chong, K., & Tuckett, D. (2013). Constructing conviction through action and narrative: how money managers manage uncertainty and the consequences for financial market functioning. Submitted to *Socio-Economic Review*: 1–26.

Keynes, J. M. (1936). *The General Theory of Employment, Interest and Money* (PaperMac edn). London: Macmillan, 1961.

Lane, D., & Maxfield, R. (2005). Ontological uncertainty and evolution. *Journal of Evolutionary Economics*, *15*: 3–50.

Taffler, R., & Tuckett, D. (2007). In the mood for instability. *Financial Times*, 20 September.

Tuckett, D. (2011). *Minding the Markets: An Emotional Finance View of Financial Instability*. Basingstoke: Palgrave Macmillan.

Tuckett, D. (2012). Financial markets are markets in stories: some possible advantages of using interviews to supplement existing economic data sources. *Journal of Economic Dynamics and Control*, *36*(8): 1077–1087.

Tuckett, D., & Nikolic, M. (2014). Conviction narrative theory: a new theory of decision-making. UCL Centre for the Study of Decision-making Uncertainty Working Paper, August.

Tuckett, D., & Taffler, R. (2003). Internet stocks as 'phantastic objects': a psychoanalytic interpretation of shareholder valuation during dot.com mania. In: *Boom or Bust? The Equity Market Crisis: Lessons for Asset Managers and Their Clients* (pp. 150–162). London: European Equity Management Association.

Tuckett, D., & Taffler, R. J. (2012). Fund management: an emotional finance perspective: Research Foundation of CFA Institute. Available at: www.cfapubs.org/toc/rf/2012/2012/2.

Tuckett, D., Smith, R. E., & Nyman, R. (2013). Tracking phantastic objects: a computer algorithmic investigation of narrative evolution in unstructured data sources. *Social Networks*, *38*(1): 121–133.

Tuckett, D., & Taffler, R. (2008): Phantastic objects and the financial market's sense of reality: a psychoanalytic contribution to the understanding of stock market instability*

A fter an initial period of enthusiasm in the earlier years of the discipline's development, and some not inconsiderable success, psychoanalysts have progressively disengaged from joining interdisciplinary attempts to use the insights gained into human psychology from their clinical work to contribute to the task of understanding wider social, political or economic phenomena.[1] Yet since standard psychoanalytic thinking significantly differs from other ways of understanding human psychology, it may have a unique contribution to make.

This paper will explore that possibility by examining a topic of current relevance; namely, perceived instability in financial markets with its very widespread consequences for human development and welfare. To understand "financial instability" (for example, the Internet bubble) we will not introduce new ways of thinking psycho-analytically; one strength of the argument we put forward is that it relies on widely accepted clinical thinking about the working of the unconscious mind, the nature of unconscious phantasy and psychic

* Originally published in *International Journal of Psychoanalysis*, 89: 389–412.

reality, the relationship between states of mind, and so on. Rather, in proposing the concept of "phantastic objects" and locating it within an established psychoanalytic theory of thinking in which reality is sensed differently in different mental states, our aim has been to frame the standard psychoanalytic understanding of human psychology in a way that is useful for applying it to social and economic questions. We have then attempted to show how it can be applied to elucidate financial markets.

Our argument is based on the ideas we developed following an analysis we undertook of the financial facts and the commentaries made on them as reported in the pages of the financial press during the Internet bubble, supplemented later by a literature review of earlier financial bubbles and a small qualitative interview study of financial professionals.[2]

Financial instability and mainstream economics

Historically, financial markets are repeatedly subject to periods when prices rise fast or decline swiftly[3] and from time to time what look like "bubbles" develop in the markets for particular assets – tulip bulbs, options to buy shares in the South Sea Company, Internet stocks, shares in emerging markets, junk or mortgage bonds, etc. At times, such as in 2007, when the market was erratic over a period of months resulting from uncertainties over the impact of the US sub-prime crisis, events on stock markets no longer merely reflect the prospects for the "real economy" – profits, incomes and employment opportunities – but affect it on a worldwide scale.

The Internet bubble, which will be our main focus, lasted for five years between 1995 and 2000. It was quite dramatic. In eighteen months between 1 October 1998 and 9 March 2000, the Dow Jones Internet index multiplied six times. In the next month it halved in value and by the end of 2002 stood at only 8 per cent of its high (see Figure 1).

Sun Microsystems (which recently changed its name to Java) is now a successful company providing software for nearly everyone's computer. Its stock price soared so that at its highest point in 1999 the total value of its shares was ten times its annual revenues (see Figure 2). After the Internet price bubble was over, Sun's chief executive set out to his shareholders how unrealistic he thought people had been:

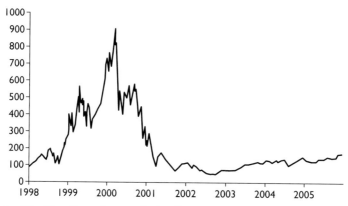

Figure 1.   The Dow Jones Internet Index (January 1998 = 100).

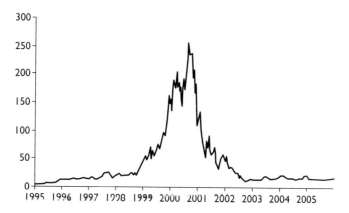

Figure 2.   The price of shares in Sun Microsystems (1995–2005).

At ten times revenues, to give you a 10-year payback, I have to pay you 100 per cent of revenues for ten straight years in dividends. That assumes I can get that by my shareholders. That assumes I have zero cost of goods sold, which is very hard for a computer company. That assumes zero expenses, which is really hard with 39,000 employees. That assumes I pay no taxes on your dividends, which is kind of illegal. And that assumes with zero R&D for the next 10 years, I can maintain the current revenue run rate. Now, having done that, would any of you like to buy my stock at $64. Do you realise how ridiculous those basic assumptions are? (Pratley, 2005, p. 25)

In mainstream economics the primary explanation for financial market bubbles or other instability is that uncertainty is introduced into individual calculation by new information. When there is news that real prospects have changed economic agents buy or sell, until prices change in line with their changed expectations of "reality". Insofar as new information is unambiguous and there are enough investors who calculate accurately and act promptly, setting aside their previous attitudes and views, a new equilibrium will be established in a consistent and efficient way. Economists have made a great deal of effort to maintain this line even where observation appears to contradict it. The general argument, although not altogether accepted (see Kay, 2003), is that, although price movements can look excessive, making markets appear inefficient and "irrational", in fact the extreme changes are perfectly consistent with the range of possible "rational" responses economic agents may have to the uncertainty introduced into their calculations by exogenous shocks. Shocks are unexpected events or new technical possibilities with implications for the real economy. They introduce uncertainty but the market actually absorbs it in an efficient way (for example, Brunnermeier, 2001; Pastor & Veronesi, 2006).

Emotion, ambiguity and uncertainty

Experience from the interviews being conducted by one of the authors suggests that uncertainty and, in particular, the difficulty of deciding what information to trust and what to ignore are indeed the main issues. This view is supported by Smith (1999), who interviewed a series of senior Wall Street participants in 1989. He found that, although they seldom admitted their uncertainties in public, these clearly emerged in his interviews. "Some . . . claim . . . to understand . . . but most, if pushed, admit they don't". He argued that this lack of understanding wasn't the result of a "shortage of explanations" but of their "abundance" (1999, p. 12). Estimations about future effects, therefore, may frequently be inherently uncertain and ambiguous.

In the psychoanalytic model we will put forward, the main explanation for market instability arises from the scope that such *ambiguity* and *uncertainty* surrounding the assessment of information provides for varying responses from economic agents. Agents can anticipate a wider range of possible future outcomes in terms of gains and losses, and in the face of uncertainty there is increased scope for emotional and unconscious phantasy to shape reactions to news. We will argue that, in the context of uncertainty and ambiguity, it is emotions and states of mind which determine the way information about reality is apprehended. Thus, willingness to take risks will vary not only when there is clear new information bearing on the "real" risks but also when there have been significant changes in the states of mind in which risks are evaluated. Such states of mind are features of the management of an everyday sense of reality in the face of uncertainty.

From a psychoanalytic point of view, we might consider that buying and selling assets involves establishing imaginative object relations to them; probably more or less ambivalent object relations. If this is the case, imaginative relations to creating or breaking emotional investment ties will be part of the evaluation of the facts in any decision to buy, sell or hold. The assessment of what is salient in any information received about a potential investment, what is real, and what the future is likely to bring, would all be influenced by both conscious and (dynamically) unconscious factors, including unconscious phantasies involving excitement, greed, anxiety and guilt, and defences against such affects because they cause psychic pain.

Freud (1911) introduced the idea that achieving the capacity to sense reality as it is, rather than as we might wish it to be, depends on the outcome of a developmental struggle between the "reality principle" and the "pleasure principle". He wrote about a developmental achievement through which a "new principle of mental functioning was thus introduced", so that "what was presented in the mind was no longer what was agreeable, but what was real, even if it happened to be disagreeable" (Freud, 1911, p. 219). The battle is never won, of course – a point that Freud saw as a new insight into something which had not previously been adequately acknowledged:

> As people grow up, then, they cease to play, and they seem to give up the yield of pleasure which they gained from playing. But whoever understands the human mind knows that hardly anything is harder for a man than to give up a pleasure which he has once experienced. Actually, we can never give anything up; we only exchange one thing for another. What appears to be a renunciation is really the formation of a substitute or surrogate. In the same way, the growing child, when he stops playing, gives up nothing but the link with real objects;

instead of *playing*, he now *phantasies*. He builds castles in the air and creates what are called *daydreams*. I believe that most people construct phantasies at times in their lives. This is a fact which has long been overlooked and whose importance has therefore not been sufficiently appreciated. (Freud 1908, p. 144)

Ideas about the way conflict between the pleasure and reality principles plays out in mental life have received much subsequent attention. A great deal of clinical experience has been accumulated and a secure literature established, describing how the perceptual conflict that gives rise to bad feelings is managed by being defended against (or split off) so that it is repressed and becomes (dynamically) unconscious. In simple terms, we realize only what we find it bearable to feel (Rickman, 1937).

A path dependent emotional trajectory but facts don't change

When we explored the main accounts of stock market bubbles (Galbraith, 1993; Kindleberger, 2000; Mackay, 1932), we were struck by the fact that they were first and foremost descriptions of an emotional sequence. Behaviour is described unambiguously in highly emotional terms. "Speculative excess, referred to concisely as a mania, and revulsion from such excess in the form of a crisis, crash, or panic can be shown to be if not inevitable, at least historically common" (Kindleberger, 2000, p. 25). In 1720 a Dutch visitor to Exchange Alley in the City of London, where South Sea stock and subscription receipts changed hands, is reported to have written home to say: "It is like nothing so much as if all the lunatics had escaped out of the madhouse all at once" (Dale et al., 2005). In other accounts such markets are regularly described at various stages as excited, excessive, euphoric, exuberant, manic, depressed, anxious, panicky, jittery, "in revulsion", ashamed, etc.

What does not seem to have been noted before, however, is that, although the timing of the emotional stages may be unpredictable, they proceed in what for a psychoanalyst is a predictable emotional direction – they are path dependent; one thing leads to another. Whether it was South Sea or Internet stock, tulip bulbs, railways, joint-stock companies in the 1920s, or junk bonds in the 1980s, in each case there was patchy excitement about an innovation leading to growing excitement, leading to manic or euphoric excitement, then turning to panic and finally resulting in blame. If the initial excitement is sustained, it invariably seems to reach towards a state of severe overconfidence in the euphoric stage (in which objections are typically treated with derision before leading to panic), and in the final stage there is invariably a wish to identify scapegoats.

We shall seek to answer two questions about this emotional path. First, why during a financial bubble does a dominant proportion of economic agents appear to become incapable of using relevant information to assess the generalized belief that something "phantastic" is happening? Second, why do anger, blame and the search for scapegoats (as in the current sub-prime 'credit crunch' crisis in the UK) erupt in the aftermath of these events, rather than guilt?

A third question is posed by a further set of observations. It is striking that the information available to economic agents to judge or price the riskiness of investments does not really change during the course of bubbles. Rather, what seems to change is the attitude of mind towards available information. While the price of stock and emotions followed their up and down path, such secure facts as were available remained largely unchanged. This point has been made by Greenspan (2007, p. 465) in his attempts to understand what was happening in 1987, when the Dow Jones lost a fifth of its value on one day. It is also clear from detailed study of what information was available during the Internet bubble. New Internet companies, whose shares were avidly accumulated when offered to the market in 1995–2000, were, if only for legal reasons, very detailed and precise in giving information about their current situations and prospects for years ahead. No new information became available that changed these prospects before the fall. At all stages companies were nearly all losing money and had no prospect of making it for many years into the future. Many pages of small print in share prospectuses spelled this out and in this sense investors always knew what they were getting: companies with few assets, little track record, forecast of losses and a lot of hope (Cassidy, 2002). Investors even seem to have thought that losing money was a positive attribute at this time for this type of business, perhaps because it meant they were investing to achieve a strong future position (Hand, 2003).

When Internet companies' share prices collapsed in March 2000 many of them had launched only months before. But after an increasing period of volatility and claim and counter-claim, sentiment towards them changed into revulsion. This was not because the case had changed. Arguments against investing in dot.com companies supported by known facts were frequent between 1996 and 2000. As in previous asset price inflations, reputable commentators and leading economists had questioned the facts or at least the assumptions and expectations implicit in the pricing of Internet stocks.[4] Such comments might have provided opportunities for those involved to reflect directly or indirectly on the facts and so to question the assumptions behind pricing. In fact such doubt was not only ignored but dismissed or met with extraordinary hyperbole.[5]

This allows us to formulate a third question: why is it that in these events the normal rules of propriety that underpin investment get broken and warnings get ignored, and why do even professional investors join in?

Towards a psychoanalytic frame: Phantastic objects

During the dot.com bubble (1995–2000) descriptions of the companies and activities associated with the Internet were full of excitement, glamour, and hyperbole. Stock markets were headline news on radio and television and the front pages of major newspapers and periodicals (Tuckett & Taffler, 2003). Looking at these accounts and those in earlier bubbles it is apparent that very clever people are engaging in novel and mysterious activities: they are creating exciting new technologies like tulip bulbs, railways or the Internet, which at the time seem to offer the possibility of substantially changing economic productivity and profitability. The opening of access to new markets, such as in Asia, similarly excites. Other new developments have been less revolutionary in terms of any hint of their direct effect on productivity, but have been novel in the sense that they were financial innovations; for example, the construction of new financial instruments (junk bonds, mortgage bonds), new ideas about efficient combinations of activities in the way businesses are run (mergers and acquisitions), the invention of new ways of holding new asset classes (hedge funds), the emergence of new types of management teams or new ways of judging what they do, and so on.

We suggest that the essence of these exciting developments can be captured by thinking of them as *phantastic objects* (Tuckett & Taffler, 2003). We derive the phrase *phantastic object* from two psychoanalytic concepts. The term *object* is used in the same sense as it is in philosophy, as a mental representation; in other words as a symbol of something but not the thing in itself.[6] The term *phantasy* (which gives rise to the term *phantastic*), as mentioned in Freud's (1908) view above, refers to an imaginary scene in which the inventor of the phantasy is a protagonist in the process of having his or her latent (unconscious) wishes fulfilled (Laplanche & Pontalis, 1973, p. 314). Thus, a *"phantastic object"* is a mental representation of something (or someone) which in an imagined scene fulfils the protagonist's deepest desires to have exactly what she wants exactly when she wants it. We might say that phantastic objects allow individuals to feel omnipotent like Aladdin (who owned a lamp which could call a genie); or like the fictional bond trader, Sherman McCoy (who felt himself a Master of the Universe [Wolfe, 1987]).[7]

Insofar as Internet stocks (tulip bulbs, South Sea shares, railways, junk bonds, mortgage bonds) are unconsciously apprehended as having the quality of phantastic objects, it is unsurprising that they generate so much excitement. As such they appear to break the usual rules of life and turn aspects of "normal" reality on its head; creating the impression that what was previously thought impossible or permanently elusive might happen after all. They are likely to create great excitement and greed which would be magnified by the worry that others might be getting them first – perhaps unconsciously reminiscent of early infantile struggles for possession of the primary objects and their attributes and also of old defeats and the opportunity to reverse them.

This hypothesis seems to us to help explain why active investors (like those in earlier asset bubbles before them) could not treat information about dot.com stock as describing shares in real companies with employees, prospects and specific calculable probabilities of finite future return, unconsciously understanding them rather as concrete opportunities to achieve omnipotent and omniscient phantasies which are usually restrained from becoming conscious reality or treated as delusions. These exciting phantasies had the power to override more realistic calculation and the judgement of the facts – a process facilitated because (as we have seen) the prospects of many companies were entirely abstract conceptions. As we see it, active investors did not "think"; rather, Internet stocks were "felt" to be a good buy. Dot.com and other "new" technology stocks came to dominate the financial markets and the financial indices, generating such extraordinary expectations that demand grew exponentially; investors competed with each other, perhaps creating further unconscious competitive excitement but certainly driving prices higher and higher.

A technical consequence of rising prices which alter the balance as to which companies are large or small relative to each other is that passive investors or those seeking to track benchmarks are also drawn into the market; the large number of index tracking funds[8] are largely forced by their mandates to own shares in popular sectors and even active professional asset managers are pressured to join in or to take the risk of being an outlier. Those who chose to stay out between 1995 and 2000 performed so badly that they either found ways to convince themselves to join in, or if they stayed true to their valuation principles then lost clients. One senior partner in a major institution interviewed in 2007 told one of us that 60 per cent of their assets under management were lost to other asset managing firms in 1999 – many billions of dollars. Such transfers had the technical effect of further amplifying trends; those assets would have been allocated to those who had performed better and so would have gone to a team prepared to invest in dot.com stocks, driving up prices even further!

A simple but ingenious piece of research provides what seems to us overwhelming evidence for the proposition that it was the idea of the Internet rather than any complex calculations of the facts about it that drove the excitement. Cooper et al. (2001) looked at the effect on the share price of companies when they changed their name. They demonstrated dramatic increases in the share price of firms which added '.com' to their names in 1998 and 1999, regardless of other factors. Specifically, they found that prices exceeded those of a control group by 63 per cent for the five days around the name-change announcement date and that this effect was independent of a company's actual level of involvement with the Internet. More detailed analysis showed how companies with non-Internet-related core businesses appearing to be Internet companies earned the greatest post-announcement returns. The excitement of association with the Internet appears to have quite overcome any detailed thinking about companies' real prospects.

A supporting story and a covering idea

When enough people perceive investment opportunities to offer the chance to possess phantastic objects and the kind of excitement just described is generated, it seems unconscious wishful phantasies can appear to be self-fulfilling, due to what are termed naturally occurring Ponzi processes (Shiller, 2000); if a market is suddenly dominated by more buyers than sellers then prices do rise, which itself appears to show the wisdom of the investment and then causes fresh waves of buying, further price rises and so on.

Markets are necessarily dominated by the active – if you don't trade by buying or selling you can't influence the price. We might think, therefore, that a selfselected group of active investors, who are more preoccupied with the search for phantastic objects than others, engage in a Ponzi process and become rewarded by it. As things go on they become more and more excited and want to engage some more. At the same time others, including the asset management pro-fessionals responsible for billions of dollars, are drawn in. Although at first they may hang back out of scepticism, they eventually convince themselves something is happening (perhaps citing a populist version of the economists' theory that markets do not lie). They then feel they can ride the wave and time their entry and exit to the market; or they may be drawn in for technical reasons (such as investment mandate requirements stating they may not be unduly underweight in a partic-ular sector since they track an index); or there may be more subtle adaptive pressures not to be left behind. One of the interviewees we spoke with recalled that during the dot.com bubble clients were anxious about fund performance and that this did create pressure for policy changes:

> And then the head of equity argued along the following lines, maybe there is something here that we're missing. I'm not sure, maybe there is, maybe we should factor in some different criteria, change some parameters to allow for something we are obviously overlooking. The market's telling us there's something we're missing. Maybe we factor in different growth rates or . . . that did actually cause us to slightly change.

Rationalization of the kind just mentioned was made easier during the dot.com bubble, as in all others, by the availability of a narrative that satisfied what Shiller (2000) calls the need for a "superficially-plausible popular theory that justifies". In fact Smelser (1962, 1998) has identified how it is necessary for leaders in a wide range of collective actions (stock market bubbles, fads, crazes and other mass movements) to supply a "generalized belief" supporting the phantasy which we might also call the manifest cover story.

Galbraith (1993) discusses the role of banking leaders and economists in helping to provide an underlying belief–narrative that made sense in the period of enthusiasm about joint-stock companies prior to the Great Crash. During the Internet bubble the cover story, which became current and apparently able to capture thinking and so perhaps to justify what was happening, was the "New Economy". The idea offered in the most influential intellectual circles was that information technology, and, in particular, the Internet, could transform productivity in the US and other economies in ways hitherto unimagined (Hall, 2000).

Cover stories appear to capture some essential sharable and simple element of the new phantastic object inventions and so provide a rationale even if it is only vaguely understood. The tone in which the new ideology of the new economy was discussed in the Internet bubble is particularly indicative. Discussions of the end of traditional methods of doing business hit headlines and today seem full of hubris. A *Time* headline (July 20, 1998) read: "Kiss Your Mall Goodbye: Online Shopping Is Faster, Cheaper and Better". An article in *Business Week* (8 February 1999), commented: "Amazon's fourth quarter sales nearly quadrupled over 1997, and compared to that, *Sears is dead*" (italics added). The cofounder of Nerve.com (*New York Magazine*, 6 March 2000) was quoted as saying: "It's incredibly powerful to feel you are one of seventeen people who really understand the world" (Grigoriadis, 2000).[9] Such irrepressible excitement about the new is characteristic of new technology bubbles (Perez, 2002).

In fact, while the bubble was still in full flow, Shiller (2000) made an extensive analysis of the rhetoric surrounding the idea and how it might increase profitability. His analysis shows that the Internet was relatively pedestrian as a new idea to increase profitability; especially compared to railways or the original freeway (motorway) system, both of which were still going to be necessary to transfer many of the Internet-ordered products. Shiller's carefully argued analysis was dismissed before the crash but proved correct soon afterwards; a further sign, perhaps, of the characteristic capacity of phantastic objects to create omnipotent and closed ways of thinking.

Changes in the financial market's sense of reality

We have seen how market thinking at the time of the dot.com bubble became saturated with the emotions felt towards Internet stock. Perceptions of reality were coloured by wishful thinking. Sceptical analysis of the claims that something completely new was happening to the economy might have provoked cautious analysis just as the rather excited and flamboyant claims being made for the new situation might have caused alarm. It is because caution, anxiety and alarm were unable to stem the flow of enthusiasm sustained by the weak cover story just discussed, that we suggest that the key to understanding such bubbles lies in the way normal reality-oriented thought, including the capacity to be anxious about potential loss in risky situations, is overridden. Active investors on a significant scale worry more about missing out on gains if they do not own a phantastic object than about losses possibly incurred from doing so.

Psychoanalytically we might understand this kind of disturbance in the market's sense of reality as the product of a group regression, where investment judgements about the risk of owning or not owning Internet stocks, based largely on individuals each assessing the situation using the reality principle, shifted towards "groupthink" (Janis, 1982) judgements based essentially on the pleasure principle. We suggest three elements are involved in this shift. First, a change takes place in the market conceived as a large group of individuals imaginatively related to each other – from work group functioning towards basic assumption group functioning (Bion, 1952). A second related change takes place in the group's sense of reality; wishful thinking – making judgements in an omnipotent mindset that makes one feel good – takes over from reality-based thinking. Third, conflict about taking on risk is eliminated or at least reduced by splitting off from awareness information that creates "bad" feelings. Together these elements allow a phantastic object to be pursued as though it is a reality and without experiencing anxiety, but at the cost of an ongoing unconscious threat that has been split off and will return. When it does re-emerge, phantastic objects become objects of revulsion.

At the heart of the psychoanalytic understanding of reality is the assumption that individuals are always in some degree of unconscious conflict; in fact, we develop a sense of mature reality by finding an individual way to accommodate the ongoing and potentially creative conflict between our wishes and our real opportunities. Much psychoanalytic theory takes as a starting point the infantile sense of wishful thinking (omnipotence). Following Freud's (1908) lead, it traces how in 'normal' development a child moves, via the medium of play and in the context of a supportive familial environment, from a sense of omnipotence towards a more or less developed awareness of the facts of life (see, for example, Fenichel, 1945; Ferenczi, 1913; Fonagy & Target, 1996; Klein, 1935; Milner, 1945; Sandler & Joffe, 1965; Winnicott, 1971 and many others). Gradually the child comes to recognize his dependence on others for satisfying wants, the limits to his personal capacity; and the facts of procreation and death (Money-Kyrle, 1971).

Again, following Freud (1908), this development towards a more realistic sense of one's capacities and place in the world is nearly always more or less of a compromise and is always only more or less believed in by the individual. One might say reality can be accepted as true "in one's heart", so to speak, or simply complied with by submitting to authority so as to reduce anxiety (see, for example, Steiner, 1996). Such theories imply that, whatever the exact outcome in any one individual, a developmental process takes place so that gradually what is felt socially and personally acceptable as "real" coincides more closely with the "true facts" of life – this is in effect what Freud had in mind with the "reality principle" and what we mean by working through the Oedipus complex.

Generalizing, we might say that what an individual knows "realistically" to be true is conscious, while what is wished for but "known" to be unrealistic, is kept secret; whether from others (more or less deliberate dissembling to avoid embarrassment, etc.) or from one's own awareness by being split off and "made" unconscious.[10]

We might summarize psychoanalytic ideas on these points by saying that they imply that the acceptance of reality is always *ambivalent*[11] and accepting the limits to personal omnipotence is a lengthy and incomplete process. Melanie Klein's (1935) concepts of the paranoid-schizoid and depressive positions deal specifically with some aspects of the process and the difficulties encountered due to intense projective and introjective mechanisms. Klein elaborates on how knowledge of ambivalent conflict is painful – creating anxiety about retaliation or experiencing guilt – and so may be avoided by splitting the perception of reality at the cost of the subject's sense of reality. Drawing on her work, we see the gradual development of a "sense of reality" as a process dependent on the capacity to reduce splitting mechanisms and to integrate conflicting feelings towards the parents in the early years.

By developing Klein's descriptions of the paranoid-schizoid and depressive positions and of the relations between them, Bion (1970) located the experience and awareness (or not) of ambivalence at the heart of psychic life. He postulates two fundamental states of mind throughout life (in Bion's notation, PS and D). We use Bion's conceptualization (italicizing his notation for this somewhat different purpose) to describe what happened to the sense of reality and states of mind in markets; we refer to the primitive (paranoid-schizoid) splitting solution to perception with the shorthand PS, while using D to designate the state of more realistic perception in which conflicts can be acknowledged.

As is well known, a D state involves giving up the feeling that one is all-powerful and all-knowing (attributed by Freud to "his majesty" the baby but a state of mind recognizable in some adults), feeling a certain amount of regret about the consequences of past actions, and a potential anticipatory feeling of depressive anxiety or guilt when contemplating potentially repeating past actions which led to failure or suffering. In a PS state all such feelings are evaded by evacuating them from awareness (projective identification) – perceiving the painful feelings as felt by others. By contrast, in a D state truth, as far as it can be seen at any one moment, can be recognized emotionally. It is important that a D state, while potentially hated and avoided in a PS state, is, once reached, often felt as a relief – offering, for example, the opportunity to repair damage and rethink errors which often leads to the better deployment of talent, or to deeper and more meaningful human relationships more free of anxiety and distrust. Shifts in the sense of reality and accompanying states of mind can be designated as $PS \rightarrow D$ or $D \rightarrow PS$ and, like the paranoid-schizoid and depressive positions, might oscillate throughout life (Britton, 1998, p. 74).

Bion (1952), it will be recalled, also made use of Freud's (1921) ideas about relations between the individual and the group, distinguishing groups as to their tendency to be Work groups or Basic assumption groups functioning in two quite different ways; both of which have a considerable effect on thinking and judging reality. It is significant that verbal communications are treated very differently in the two types of group functioning: "We have been forced to the conclusion that verbal exchange is only understood by the W[ork] group. In proportion as the group is dominated by a basic assumption *verbal communication is important only as a vehicle for sound*" (Bion, 1952, p. 244, italics added),

This implies that the information gained from activities like data analysis and detailed company research would be treated differently by the two different types of group; in a Work group it can be used by individuals in the service of real thought (in the usual symbolic reflective sense), but in the Basic assumption group the accumulation of information is used not for thought but to feel good (Bion, 1952, p. 245).

If we return now to the way the sense of reality in financial markets appears to change during an asset price bubble, we suggest that, to the extent that there is a shared belief in the existence of a phantastic object as a real possibility, a Basic assumption group has formed. The group is subject to wishful thinking – making judgements omnipotently that feel good – which takes over from reality-based thinking, leading to a Basic assumption rather than Work group approach to information. A PS state of mind is also established in which conflict about taking on risk is split off from awareness so that information is evaluated only to create "good" excited feelings. A phantastic object can now be enthusiastically pursued as though it was a reality, and the view that it is much less risky to invest than to miss out on investing in dot.com stocks can become dominant. In this state the judgements of economic agents are based primarily on their excited and wishful feelings and they disregard the countervailing anxiety which would otherwise be awakened by traditional valuation methods. The shared unconscious phantasy (the existence of phantastic objects) is legitimated through a cover story – for example, a new economy which does not work like the old.

Dominated by the pursuit of such excitement and in a PS state of mind, potentially persecuting and frustrating opposing views could be, as we have seen, ignored or dismissed. In this state of mind neither sceptical comment nor the facts of companies' own detailed warnings of losses for some years to come had sufficient impact to cause caution. Active economic agents did not "feel" interested. The state of mind in which active investors eventually made their judgements can be characterized as anti-thought, or, to use another of Bion's ideas, governed by −K (Bion, 1962). −K contrasts with K, where the relationship to an object in unconscious phantasy is imbued with curiosity and enquiry. The distinguishing point is that, while in both types of object-relationship there can be a great deal of preoccupation or excitement with the object, in −K the object itself is of no interest or concern except to be possessed. This is a form of greedy relationship to an object characteristic of the PS state of mind. Concern for the used object is split-off from consciousness, existing only as unconscious anxiety.

When the dominant mental state within the market was PS it was impossible to reflect upon the true nature of what was being wished for. Conflict in a PS state is persecuting so doubts, objections, and anxieties are not salient; they are unconscious and kept unconscious because they are painful. This represents a reversal of the usual developmental trajectory towards accepting painful conflict and where necessary disappointment, which is associated with the D state of mind.

New economy: New rules

According to the view just set out, belief in the real availability of phantastic objects turns reality upside down. Beliefs otherwise thought unrealistic become commonplace and a new PS reality is born. In the dot.com period the new enterprises were widely discussed and seriously "analysed" as subject to different "new" rules. The implication was that the usual developmental trajectory that an individual's sense of reality could take might be reversible – instead of gradually giving up the conviction that one is all-powerful there is a new belief that omnipotent wishful fulfilment may really be on offer. Euripides describes such scenes in the *Bacchae*.

As a matter of fact the dot.com entrepreneurs were youthful and as such (and as indicated by some of the more flamboyant quotations earlier) apparently able to reverse the normal pecking order of the generations as well as to dismiss the "outdated" methods of thought accumulated by their experienced superiors. Kay (2003) makes the point that the behaviour of economic agents is adaptive to their (emotional) environment. If a "new reality" starts to dawn, then valuation procedures within groups change to fit it.

In December 1998 Henry Blodget, a journalist who had found a job as a securities analyst at a small investment bank, announced that shares in Amazon.com were worth at least $400 each. The price was then already $250. Jonathan Cohen, the analyst at the prestigious Merrill Lynch, using traditional criteria, countered with the suggestion (subsequently shown to be correct) that $50 was more realistic. But within a month Amazon shares had soared beyond $400 and, as Kay put it,

> "Blodget soared with it: he succeeded to Cohen's job" (Kay, 2003, p. 208).

The rules governing how securities analysts calculated the value of Internet companies underwent further adaptation. Since conventional methods of valuation showed them to be very risky investments at high prices, the idea was not to concentrate on such "old" economy measures as earnings, cash flows or dividends but to use "new" economy concepts instead: such as profits net of most costs; revenue growth; mind share; website activity measured in terms of clicks, reach and stickiness; and numbers of visitors times lifetime value of a customer. This shift was well described as it was happening but not to any effect: "Analysts are slicing, dicing and torturing numbers until they can be moulded into what might pass for a rationale to back up a table pounding investment recommendation", two critics suggested at the time (Laderman & Smith, 1998, pp. 120–122). On the excited side, it was claimed that the Internet had ". . . introduced a brave new world for valuation methodologies . . . we believe that we have entered a new valuation zone" (Meeker, 1997, p. 1).

What happened in the euphoria period is common to other periods of basic assumption group pressure. One US investment banker interviewed put into words what many others implied. He and his senior colleagues had felt pressurized, he said, "to conform with the demands of younger colleagues during this period – as regards investment policy, house rules, dress codes, etc." He reported there was even a word coined for not going along with it all: you would be "Amazoned" – left out in the cold, made obsolete, like "old" economy blue chip companies.

There is some evidence those in authority were taken by the mood of rebellion. For example, in its e-commerce policy paper in the summer of 1997 the Clinton administration decided a hands-off attitude to the Internet was in the US's strategic interest. Clinton himself is reported to have "felt" the economists he consulted were wrong (Greenspan, 2007, pp. 170–171), and one of the most influential proponents of taking seriously the New Economy doctrine was the then Federal Reserve Bank Chairman, Alan Greenspan (1997). Both may have thus have lent the idea, more than they realized, both authoritative and moral legitimation.[12]

Certainly rules were modified opportunistically over a wide range of financial activity – as, for instance, in the culture of risk control in investment banks – as it now appears was also happening prior to 2007 when banks could not resist the extra yield on mortgage securities and Collaterized Debt Obligations. Before the Internet companies arrived, it had been usual for top investment banks to avoid high-risk new companies, to protect their valuable "reputational capital". But not this time. Offers to purchase shares in new Internet companies (IPOs) were eventually over 40 per cent more likely to be underwritten by one of the six most prestigious underwriters than by others (Schultz and Zaman, 2001) presumably because they did not think them risky.

Panic: The return of the repressed?

The crash that occurred in April 2000 was dramatic, like the earlier ones in financial history. What was once highly valued became quickly shunned and many Internet share certificates soon became less useful than wallpaper. The "new economy" and all its valuation metrics were now mostly dismissed as "fantasy". As in other bubbles investors did not gradually become more realistic; their valuations were suddenly and almost universally *felt* to be hopelessly unrealistic so that many more sellers than buyers were to be found and prices fell exponentially.

Whereas Internet stocks had been phantastic objects they were now reviled ones; stigmatized and felt to be a massive liability. The same research team who had demonstrated the positive effect of adding the .com suffix in 1999 now showed the benefit of taking it away (Cooper et al., 2005). They showed how investors reacted very positively to these name removals with abnormal positive returns of around 70 per cent for the 60 day period surrounding the announcement day. Their work shows that the market was still operating more on feelings than careful thought and confirmed perceptions at the time.

It does not require any psychoanalytic thinking to describe the crash as panic or to predict what people were likely to do when faced with a sudden threat to the value of their investments. But a psychoanalyst can perhaps add to understanding by drawing attention to a path dependent process. Holding financial assets necessarily establishes ambivalent unconscious phantasy relationships, which can then be managed in a D or PS state of mind, and in bubbles a PS sense of reality derived from splitting comes to dominate. Then, in the crash, investors suffer the return of the repressed. Knowledge that their investments were based on very risky assumptions had always been there; but such doubts were unconscious while an idealized love affair was in progress. Investors became conscious of the knowledge and feelings hitherto split off, including perhaps the anxiety stirred by their previous activities. They were now forced to own the experience of risk and to notice facts that had always been there. Moreover, "cover" stories now failed to give support; if doubts were now to be subjected to thought such theories were not convincing. The phantastic object was now an unconscious persecutory object.

It seems unlikely that we will ever be able to say why a crash happens when it does, just as in psychoanalytic treatment it is by no means easy to know what it is that causes a patient finally to take in difficult interpretations and then to work them through rather than to leave treatment and fail. Because hindsight is a great provider of wisdom, it is worth mentioning that several interviewees mentioned that, even in the few weeks before the bubble burst, a significant number of leading investment managers (or the institutions they worked for) were sacked or nearly sacked by their clients for underperformance; because they had not been prepared to invest in dot.com stocks.

Blame as a signal of unconscious guilt and shame

So far we have proposed that, during an asset price bubble, it is economic agents' sense of reality that shifts first in favour of and then

in revulsion towards phantastic objects and that this change in sentiment occurs without new information.

Once the bubble bursts a new sense of reality can come about but
this is not necessarily based on D, that is to say, the acceptance of
conflictual and limited reality. A period of what might be called
bargaining with reality can take place in which it is not only the pleasure principle that must be relinquished as an organizing principle for
investment but also the P sense of reality; to give up the latter requires
a mourning process in which integration of split-off and conflicting
thoughts and feelings towards the phantastic object must take place.

In fact observation suggests that after a crash the euphoria stage of
financial bubbles generally gives way to denial, to anger, and then to
paranoid efforts to find scapegoats. Typically there is rather little real
working through or recognition of responsibility and guilt. Insofar as
the incidents receive formal forensic investigation, it tends to focus on
external sources (exogenous shocks) and on the "shakers" and
"movers" promoting the objects that once caused such excitement.

After the collapse a series of long articles in the *New York Times*
variously blamed Wall Street (31 December 2000), corporate "propa-
ganda" (18 March 2001), investment banks (15 April 2001) and
conflicts of interest (27 May 2001). Blame was also successfully laid in
the courts. A $1.4bn global settlement was extracted by US regulators
from 10 leading Wall Street investment banks in April 2003, and
lawsuits were taken out against the main Internet analysts at Merrill
Lynch, Salomon, and Credit Suisse First Boston A similar process is
now observable in the 2007 UK banking crisis that has followed the
sub-prime debacle.

History teaches us to expect blame rather than analysis in such
situations. Mackay in his discussion of the outcome of the South Sea
Bubble notes what he called the innumerable public meetings and
inquests held in "every town of the British empire". There was a good
deal of 'praying for vengeance' on the company directors but:
"Nobody seemed to imagine that the nation itself was as culpable as
the South Sea Company. Nobody blamed the credulity and avarice of
the people . . . or the infatuation which had made the multitude run
their heads . . . These things were never mentioned" (Mackay, 1932,
p. 72).

Similarly, Galbraith (1993) describes how repeated inquests and
investigations in other bubbles attend to everything but the basic

issue: how and why did otherwise sensible people get caught up? He finds it common that prominent figures turn from being perceived as financial geniuses into immoral knaves and are then prosecuted. External exogenous shocks or foreign influences are the candidates to be implicated.

From a psychoanalytic point of view the presence of denial, anger and then blame (rather than guilt) indicates the continuance of a P rather than a D sense of reality: whereas criticism of Internet companies was projected and denied during the upside, it is now the old love of the companies which is disowned and projected. In such a state of mind individuals are free to feel angry and hurt and to blame those who seduced them. The companies themselves are hated and stigmatized and it remains difficult to value them realistically.

We have suggested that investing in assets of all kinds is usefully conceived as creating an unconscious and necessarily ambivalent phantasy object relationship, where the experience of dependence leads to potential anxiety and distrust. When these emotions are split off they can return with a vengeance when things go wrong, attacking the individual with bad feelings. Blaming others is unlikely to help participants to come to terms with their experience or learn from it; this requires a D state and acceptance of the pain of feeling guilt.

A psychoanalytic understanding of financial bubbles

Financial market bubbles mainly occur when new developments appear to offer potentially exceptional yields to investors, often at times of promised technological changes which make future developments increasingly difficult to predict (for a discussion, see Perez, 2002). The foregoing analysis shows how a psychoanalytic understanding of emotional processes can throw light on the behaviour of economic agents in these circumstances. It shows why, even if economic agents try to adopt the consistent utility-maximizing behaviour which economists model when the circumstances are propitious, they are unable to do so effectively when faced with ambiguous information which creates strong ambivalent feelings.

We have argued that information is processed differently when groups of economic agents come to share an unconscious belief in the existence of what we have termed a phantastic object. Through imaginative identification with each other they become a Basic assumption group united by their belief in the phantastic object and its supporting cover story and operating within a PS sense of reality; in which the conflicts otherwise caused by risky behaviour, anxiety and doubt, or anything that could give rise to "bad feelings", are split off so that information about them is non-salient. Once deemed "real" and sanctioned within a social group, phantastic objects appear to offer the opportunity to break the rules of usual life and so turn "normal" reality on its head; creating the impression that what was previously thought impossible or given up as a possibility might happen after all. Not everyone in a market has to be a believer. The active behaviour of the believing group is sufficient to move prices and to become self-rewarding, feeding the belief they are really in the presence of the phantastic object which leads to growing excitement and a belief in a more and more contagious new reality. When the bubble bursts this is not due to new information; rather it seems the dizzy heights reached create an accumulation of split-off anxiety recognized in past descriptions as "uneasiness, apprehension, tension, stringency, pressure, uncertainty, ominous conditions, fragility" (Kindleberger, 2000, p. 95); this ushers in a period of volatile oscillation before the return of the repressed anxieties and the crash. This analysis offers some answers to the three questions about financial market bubbles posed earlier.

First, it suggests why during a financial bubble a dominant proportion of economic agents appear to become incapable of using relevant information to assess the generalized belief that something 'phantastic' is happening. It is because they have become part of a Basic assumption group operating with a PS sense of reality and so able to share a feeling that phantastic objects are actually real.

Second, it explains why once 'basic assumption' mentality takes over, those who do use known facts to make "rational" and cautious choices tend to lose their jobs; fear of which causes others to "adapt" and so fuels the process. Only when the anxieties produced by available information can no longer be made unconscious do economic actors within Basic assumption groups become overwhelmed by "jitters"; at this point their ambivalent relationship shifts in a reverse direction; the same information is now considered to be nothing but "bad" news.

Third, it helps explain why anger and blame rather than guilt erupt in the aftermath of these events. Feeling guilt requires painful working through of the truth of events which is often avoided; certainly within basic assumption groups and so long as individuals' sense of reality is governed by a PS rather than D state of mind. A D state of mind is not reached out of panic and compliance; it requires mourning.

Economic theory as an institutional frame

We suggest, tentatively, that the psychoanalytic understanding just offered can contribute to a more complete interdisciplinary theory of financial market instability making better sense of economic agents' experiences; in part by directing attention to some institutional features of these markets which may predispose them to develop states of mind and group functioning of the kinds discussed.

Two such institutional features will be discussed. The first concerns the nature of theories about their work that economic agents develop, and how far these equip them to deal with the problems that their emotions and the inherent uncertainty of their task necessarily force them to experience. The second concerns the arrangements within financial market institutions to assess and manage personal performance, including when losses are incurred for clients. Some institutional arrangements may be more or less conducive to processes of mourning and learning from experience, for example. We will close by reviewing some preliminary ideas.

The theories with which individuals explain to themselves what they do and how they do it are part of the institutional arrangements which help them to work competently and to manage the stresses of work. Whereas a psychoanalyst will to a considerable extent define his or her task on the basis of his or her private and more or less conscious understanding and internalization of psychoanalytic theory (see Canestri, 2006; Tuckett et al., 2008), an economic agent in a financial market will do the same but based on economic theory. Formal economic theory, therefore, is part of the institutional arrangements framing how individuals "should" perform their market roles (Mackenzie, 2005). In this respect, based on our observations about the Internet bubble, mainstream economics and finance theories may be problematic because they misdirect attention away from the issues economic agents must ordinarily face in financial markets in several important ways.

First, mainstream economic theory (unlike its Keynesian variant, see, for example, Minsky, 1982) conceives of markets as composed of unattached and un-related individuals operating in an institution-free world. That might be an acceptable characterization of a Work group. However, financial markets frequently resemble large Basic assumption groups acting almost without individuality.

Second, mainstream theories do not help economic agents with the problem of how to make quick decisions with too much ambiguous and uncertain information. The institutional context we found professional fund managers describing, when they were interviewed in 2007, was one in which interpreting information in financial markets was a matter of selection from conflicting signals. Situations where things were straightforward either did not occur or were uninteresting – because everyone agreed on the price and there was no investment opportunity. Rather they had routinely to manage two different orders of essentially irresolvable uncertainty that necessarily posed emotional conflict. One set of uncertainties was caused by unavoidable information asymmetries as they tried to sort out the mass of ambiguous information with which they were bombarded at the moment of decision-making. Another set was determined by the fact that, however well they know the present, the future is inherently unknowable. Respondents had to predict both how the underlying enterprises they wanted to invest in would do in the future and how other people would predict as well (see, also, Keynes, 1936, p. 156). They then had to wait and see what the necessarily unpredictable future would bring. Nothing done in the present can quantify that risk or remove that uncertainty. Because investors need to predict the future behaviour of firms and their customers, competitors, future human innovation, and the responses to information about all this among others in financial markets, they are constantly uncertain and anxious about their decisions to buy, hold or sell assets. Decisions will always involve some degree of balancing hope and risk – including the risk of getting it wrong and then of having to pay the price. This leads to the temptation to split off the good "exciting" experience of hope from the bad "painful" risk of loss.

Third, mainstream economic theory reduces emotion to the irrational. It thus implausibly and unhelpfully ignores the functional role of emotion in good decision-making. In recent years a weight of argument has been assembled to suggest that the model of consistent calculating economic man is an unhelpful abstraction at odds with empirical descriptions of how anyone makes effective decisions (see Berezin, 2005; Gigerenzer, 2007). The traditional contrast between rational economic man and irrational or emotional decision-making ignores not only psychoanalytic and other empirical experience but also growing neurobiological evidence that emotion, far from being a distraction for effective decision-making, has been evolved to be useful in making complex decisions quickly and adaptively (Bechara & Damasio, 2005; Gigerenzer, 2007). The important point is that ignoring emotion in economic theories creates an institutional context where formal attention cannot be given to it; in these circumstances it is very likely defended against and split off, probably in dysfunctional ways. This is an area for further research.

Fourth, through the doctrine of general equilibrium (the idea that the 'hidden hand' of the market always produces the best possible outcomes providing individuals are left free to pursue self-interest), economic theory enables individuals to split off the consequences of responsibility for decision-making; it is the market not individuals which can somehow be held accountable. This may help to explain why little forensic examination is given to the aftermath of financial crises beyond seeking to place blame. A theory leaving out emotion, defensive behaviour and institutions will not facilitate working through guilt and developing a D state of mind in which to make future uncertain and anxiety-inducing decisions. We might also expect that the greedy pursuit of individual interest in a PS or D state of mind is rather different. In a PS state longer term consequences can be split off, but not in a D state. Currently financial markets are notoriously short-term.

Evaluating performance

The way economic agents are rewarded for their performance in financial markets is another important part of the institutional context in which they work. Earlier we described how, during the Internet bubble, fears about under-performance and subtle adaptation brought in even the "unbelievers". The way performance evaluation works may create emotional conflicts for economic agents which, if left unaddressed, may worsen market instability in at least three ways.

First, the industry is founded on a contradiction. The professional asset management industry is very large, global and highly competitive. Asset managers sell their approach by pointing to past performance while at the same time they advise would-be customers, using small print, "past performance is no guide to future performance". The contradiction frames the institutional situation in which portfolio managers find themselves as they try to think about their work; the size of the sums they can obtain to manage determines their fees and their performance determines the assets they get asked to manage. At the same time, the evidence as to whether a fund manager or any other investor can systematically and consistently outperform the market except by chance is largely negative (for example, Malkiel, 2003, p. 268). This situation undoubtedly creates emotional conflict but may also create a PS state of mind. Managers who survive may do so because they take more risks than average and get lucky – the others who take equivalent risk but were not so lucky lose their jobs. If so, there is a reward for splitting. Adapting expressions used by Arrow (1963), investment management may be based on adverse selection and moral hazard (both rewarding a PS rather than D sense of reality). If so, this is likely to contribute to ongoing financial instability.

Second, the asset management industry, like the wider banking community, has taken the view that it can actually measure risk. Following a number of financial scandals and administrative reforms (Clark and Thrift, 2005), risk in investment portfolios is now measured. This is done by calculating the historical variability of the price of all assets in a portfolio and then calculating an overall risk coefficient represented as volatility. This approach can be regarded as impression management (Goffman, 1959) or part of the way investment professionals configure their image as so-to-speak scientists; thus creating formal ways to distance themselves from the origins of the industry in gambling and speculating (Preda, 2005). It is controversial because the measurements, which appear to predict the future precisely, use inevitably arbitrary selections of past data to do so. The approach may discipline economic agents and make them think about the positions they build up, but cannot overcome the fact that the future is inherently uncertain (Pixley, 2004; Taleb, 2005). This logical point was demonstrated in the summer of 2007, when after financial markets behaved in "extraordinary" ways, some investment managers were to be found complaining there has been more than one "25 sigma" event in a week.[13] In terms of the psychoanalytic ideas we have been developing, the question would be whether risk measurement is implemented in a PS or a D state – as part of a Work group approaching a problem to create more thought, or a Basic assumption group making itself feel safe by trying not to think. In the latter case risk measures could function like reassuring noise, making anxieties unconscious pending the return of the repressed.

Third, the way performance measurement is used to reward managers or funds may have some significant consequences. Performance is generally defined in relative terms; by comparing any one manager against a benchmark index which is the average of all others in a given category over a set period of time. Because computers make such performance easy to calculate on a moment by moment basis managers can be compared to their peers minute by minute. This raises the question of whether short-term performance provides any guide to longer term performance (Taleb, 2005) but also, and more significantly, how long managers, their superiors or their clients can tolerate performance below the average – clearly an emotional question involving trust and distrust. What one interviewee called the "tyranny" of the benchmark creates continual pressure and stress, potentially directing everyone to short-term results and making the ongoing relation to assets fraught. This structural situation makes it hard to stick to unfashionable strategies if they do not produce quick results and will tend to create benchmark hugging – one explanation for the pressure for the unbelievers to join in when a phantastic object makes waves.

Notes

1. Compare the historical account of the major role psychoanalysts played in aspects of the second world war and its aftermath (King, 1989) with more recent (themselves quite rare) efforts to explore way it can contribute to socio-economic or political situations – for example. Altman (2005), Eizirik (1997) or Kernberg (2003). An exception is Steinberg, 1991.
2. The first-named author is currently conducting an in-depth study of 50 experienced asset or portfolio equity managers working for major asset management houses in Asia, continental Europe, the UK and the US.

Some anecdotal comments from this study or the pilot interviews with senior figures in the asset management industry will be used to support some parts of the argument, where it appears that what he has been told is reliable and substantiated by more than one respondent. The basic thesis has been presented to financial professionals and published in two professional directed publications (see Tuckett & Taffler, 2003; Taffler & Tuckett, 2007a, 2007b). The interview study was made possible by a 2007 Leverhulme research fellowship. *[This was at the time of writing the 2008 paper; see chapter introduction for update on outcomes.]*

3. The value of all the shares on the US stock market (measured by the Dow Jones Industrial average) can fall precipitously; 90 per cent between 1928 and 1929 causing widespread unemployment and social and political dislocation; 26 per cent on one day on 19 October 1987 (only to recover half that amount two days later); 7 per cent on 17 September 2001 (the first day markets were open after the terrorist attacks).

4. There were articles expressing serious doubt in each of the five years – see Tuckett & Taffler, 2003. As an example: Barron's (30 August 1999) "Qué pasa? Quién sabe?" begins "We all know that evaluating Internet stocks encompasses less science than does opting whether to hit or hold in Atlantic City . . ."

5. Mary Meeker wrote: "The difference is that real values are being created. Tulip bulbs would not fundamentally change the way the companies do business" (Cassidy, 2002, p. 217). Henry Blodget (1999) was still more effusive: "With these types of investments, we would also argue that the 'real' risk is not losing some money – it is missing a much bigger upside."

6. An object in this sense, therefore, is not limited to a physical object. It could be a representation of a thing or a person or a relationship but it could also represent just an idea.

7. Or indeed like the successful bond traders at Solomon brothers who thought of themselves as "big swinging dicks" (Lewis, 1989).

8. Tracking funds are obliged to invest in the same proportion of different stocks as contained in the index being tracked. These proportions are dynamically updated by price changes.

9. The point is made in this article that the original entrepreneurs interviewed had little genius for business or computer programming but did have "the kind of finely tuned pop culture antennae needed to be in the right place at the right time" (Grigoriadis, 2000).

10. The way the bond trader, Sherman McCoy, struggled with voicing his belief his success showed he was a Master of the Universe is masterfully described by Tom Wolfe (1987).

11. The ideas set out here were arrived at independently. But Neil Smelser, a sociologist also trained as a psychoanalyst, has made the case for using ambivalence rather than rationality as an assumption governing economic and social analysis (Smelser, 1998).

12. Shiller (2005, pp. 207 et seq.) has suggested authoritative official pronouncements at such moments could be an important way to prevent the development of price bubbles.

References

Altman, N. (2005). Manic society: toward the depressive position. *Psychoanalytic Dialogues, 15*: 321–346.

Arrow, K. J. (1963). Uncertainty and the welfare economics of medical care. *American Econonomic Revue, 53*: 941–973.

Bechara, A., & Damasio, A. R. (2005). The somatic marker hypothesis: a neural theory of economic decision. *Games and Economic Behaviour, 52*: 336–372.

Berezin, M. (2005). Emotions and the economy. In: N. J. Smelser & R. Swedberg (Eds). *Handbook of Economic Sociology* (2nd edn) (pp. 109–127. New York: Russell Sage Foundation and Princeton University Press.

Bion, W. R. (1952). Group dynamics: a re-view. *International Journal of Psychoanalysis, 33*: 235–247.

Bion, W. R. (1962). *Learning from Experience*. London: Tavistock.

Bion, W. R. (1970). *Attention and Interpretation: A Scientific Approach to Insight in Psycho-analysis and Groups*. London: Tavistock.

Blodget, H. (1999). Internet/Electronic commerce report. Merrill Lynch, 9 March.

Britton, R. S. (1998). Before and after the depressive position Ps(n)->D(n) ->Ps(n+1). In: *Belief and Imagination: Explorations in Psychoanalysis* (pp. 69–81). London: Routledge.

Brunnermeier, M. (2001). *Asset Pricing under Asymmetric Information: Bubbles, Crashes, Technical Analysis, and Herding*. Oxford: Oxford University Press.

Canestri, J. (Ed.) (2006). *Psychoanalysis: From Practice to Theory*. London: Wiley.

Cassidy, J. (2002). *Dot.con: The Greatest Story Ever Told*. London: Allen Lane/Penguin.

Clark, G. L., & Thrift, N. (2005). The return of bureaucracy: managing dispersed knowledge in global finance. In: K. Knorr Certina & A.

Preda (Eds.), *The Sociology of Financial Markets*. Oxford: Oxford University Press.

Cooper, M. J., Dimitrov, O., & Rau, P. R. (2001). A rose.com by any other name. *Journal of Finance*, *56*(6): 2371–2388.

Cooper, M. J., Khorana, A., Osobov, I., Patel, A., & Rau, P. R. (2005). Managerial action in response to a market downturn: valuation effects of name changes in the dot.com decline. *Journal of Corporate Finance*, *11*(1–2): 319–335.

Dale, R. S., Johnson, J. E. V., & Tang, L. (2005). Financial markets can go mad: evidence of irrational behaviour during the South Sea Bubble. *Economic History Review*, *58*(2): 233–271.

Eizirik, C. L. (1997). Psychoanalysis and culture: some contemporary challenges. *International Journal of Psychoanalysis*, *78*: 789–800.

Fenichel, O. (1945). The means of education. *Psychoanalytic Study of the Child*, *1*: 281–292.

Ferenczi, S. (1913). Stages in the development of the sense of reality. In: *First Contributions to Psychoanalysis* (pp. 212–239). London: Hogarth, 1952.

Fonagy, P., & Target, M. (1996). Playing with reality: I. Theory of mind and the normal development of psychic reality. *International Journal of Psychoanalysis*, *77*: 217–233.

Freud, S. (1908). Creative writers and day-dreaming. *S.E.*, *9*: 141–153. London: Hogarth.

Freud, S. (1911). Formulations regarding the two principles of mental functioning. *S.E.*, *12*: 213–226. London: Hogarth.

Freud, S. (1921). *Group Psychology and the Analysis of the Ego*. *S.E.*, *18*: 65–144. London: Hogarth.

Galbraith, J. K. (1993). *A Short History of Financial Euphoria*. New York: Penguin.

Gigerenzer, G. (2007). *Gut Feelings*. London: Allen Lane/Penguin.

Goffman, E. (1959). *The Presentation of Self in Everyday Life*. New York: Doubleday Anchor.

Greenspan, A. (1997). Monetary policy testimony and report to congress, July 22nd.

Greenspan, A. (2007). *The Age of Turbulence: Adventures in a New World*. London: Allen Lane/Penguin.

Grigoriadis, V. (2000). Silicon Alley 10003: Long before the suits logged on, a small group of prep-school slackers had faith in the Web. Now they're the alley's establishment. *New York Magazine*, March 6, 2000 (http://nymag.com/nymetro/news/media/internet/2285/).

Hall, R. E. (2000). E-capital: the link between the stock market and the labor market in the 1990s. *Brookings Papers on Economic Activity*, 2: 73–102.

Hand, J. R. M. (2003). Profits, losses and the non-linear pricing of Internet stocks. In: J. R. M. Hand & B. Lev (Eds.), *Intangible Assets: Values, Measures and Risks* (pp. 248–268). Oxford: Oxford University Press.

Janis, I. (1982). *Groupthink* (2nd edn). Boston, MA: Houghton Mi_in.

Kay, J. (2003). *The Truth about Markets*. London: Penguin.

Kernberg, O. F. (2003). Sanctioned social violence: a psychoanalytic view. Part I. *International Journal of Psychoanalysis*, *84*: 683–698. (See also Part 2, 953–968.)

Keynes, J. M. (1936). *The General Theory of Employment, Interest and Money* (PaperMac edn). London: Macmillan, 1961.

Kindleberger, C. P. (2000). *Manias, Panics and Crashes* (4th edn). New York: Wiley.

King, P. H. (1989). Activities of British psychoanalysts during the Second World War and the influence of their inter-disciplinary collaboration on the development of psychoanalysis in Great Britain. *International Review of Psychoanalysis*, *16*: 15–32.

Klein, M. (1935). A contribution to the psychogenesis of manic-depressive states. *International Journal of Psychoanalysis*, *16*: 145–174.

Knorr Certina, K., & Preda, A. (Eds.) (2005). *The Sociology of Financial Markets*. Oxford: Oxford University Press.

Laderman, M., & Smith, G. (1998). Internet stocks: what's their real worth? New methods show why the bets are so risky. *Business Week*, *3608*, 14 December.

Lane, D., & Maxfield, R. (2005). Ontological uncertainty and evolution. *Journal of Evolutionary Economics*, *15*: 3–50.

Laplanche, J., & Pontalis, J.-B. (1973). *The Language of Psychoanalysis*, D. Nicholson-Smith (Trans.). New York: Norton.

Lewis, M. (1989). *Liar's Poker*. London: Coronet.

Mackay, C. (1932). *Memoirs of Extraordinary Popular Delusions and the Madness of Crowds*. London: Wordsworth Reference.

Mackenzie, D. (2005). How a superportfolio emerges: long-term capital management and the sociology of arbitrage. In: K. Knorr Certina & A. Preda (Eds.), *The Sociology of Financial Markets*. Oxford: Oxford University Press.

Malkiel, B. (2003). *A Random Walk down Wall Street* (revised edn). New York: Norton.

Meeker, M. (1997). US and the Americas investment research, Morgan Stanley Dean Whitter, September 16.

Milner, M. (1945). Some aspects of phantasy in relation to general psychology. *International Journal of Psychoanalysis, 26*: 143–152.

Minsky, H. P. (1982). *Can 'It' Happen Again? Essays on Instability and Finance*. New York: Sharpe.

Money-Kyrle, R. (1971). The aim of psychoanalysis. *International Journal of Psychoanalysis, 52*: 103–106.

Pastor, L., & Veronesi, P. (2006). Was there a NASDAQ bubble in the late 1990s? *Journal of Financial Economics, 81*: 61–100.

Perez, C. (2002). *Technological Revolutions and Financial Capital: The Dynamics of Bubbles and Golden Ages*. Cheltenham: Edward Elgar.

Pixley, J. (2004). *Emotions in Finance*. Cambridge: Cambridge University Press.

Pratley, N. (2005). Google shares are a bubble waiting to pop. *Guardian*, 10 June 2004.

Preda, A. (2005). The investor as a cultural figure of global capitalism. In: K. Knorr Certina & A. Preda (Eds.), *The Sociology of Financial Markets* (pp. 00–00). Oxford: Oxford University Press.

Rickman, J. (1937). On 'unbearable' ideas and impulses. *American Journal of Psychology, 50*: 248–253. Reprinted in: *Selected Contributions to Psychoanalysis*. London: Hogarth, 1957.

Sandler, J., & Joffe, W. G. (1965). Notes on obsessional manifestations in children. *Psychoanalytic Study of the Child, 20*: 425–438.

Schultz, P., & Zaman, M. (2001). Do the individuals closest to Internet firms believe they are overvalued? *Journal of Financial Econonomics, 59*(3): 347–381.

Shiller, R. J. (2000). *Irrational Exuberance*. Princeton, NJ: Princeton University Press.

Shiller, R. J. (2005). *Irrational Exuberance* (2nd edn). Princeton, NJ: Princeton University Press.

Smelser, N. (1962). *Theory of Collective Behaviour*. New York: Free Press of Glencoe.

Smelser, N. (1998). The rational and the ambivalent in the social sciences. *American Sociological Review, 63*(1): 1–16.

Smith, C. W. (1999). *Success and Survival on Wall Street: Understanding the Mind of the Market* (2nd edn). Lanham, MD: Rowman & Littlefield.

Steinberg, B. S. (1991). Psychoanalytic concepts in international politics: the role of shame. *International Review of Psychoanalysis, 18*: 65–85.

Steiner, J. (1996). Revenge and resentment in the 'Oedipus situation'. *International Journal of Psychoanalysis, 77*: 433–443.

Taffler, R., & Tuckett, D. (2007a). Emotional finance: understanding what drives investors. *Professional Investor*, Autumn: 26–27.

Taffler, R., & Tuckett, D. (2007b). In the mood for instability. *Financial Times*, 20 September.

Taleb, N. N. (2005). *Fooled by Randomness* (revised edn). London: Penguin.

Tuckett, D., & Taffler, R. (2003). Internet stocks as 'phantastic objects': a psychoanalytic interpretation of shareholder valuation during dot.com mania. In: *Boom or Bust? The Equity Market Crisis: Lessons for Asset Managers and Their Clients* (pp. 150–162). London: European Equity Management Association.

Tuckett, D., Basile, R., Birksted Breen, D., Bohm, T., Denis, P., Ferro, A., Hinz, H., Jemstedt, A., Mariotti, P., & Schubert, J. (2008). *Psychoanalysis Comparable and Incomparable: The Evolution of a Method to Describe and Compare Psychoanalytic Approaches*. London: Routledge, New Library of Psychoanalysis.

Winnicott, D. W. (1971). *Playing and Reality*. London: Tavistock.

Wolfe, T. (1987). *The Bonfire of the Vanities*. London: Picador.

CHAPTER FIVE

Love, money, and identity

Anca Carrington

Introduction

In his exploration of the lives and choices of the famously rich, Wiseman (1974) recognises "a greed of a peculiarly elemental kind", that is, "the greed for more than the subject needs or the object can give" (p 46). This is very much in the spirit of Klein's (1935) understanding of greed, fundamentally linked to primitive aggression, originating in the oral stage of development, where the infant pursues "a hungry, destructive introjection of the frustrating breast" (Akhtar, 2009, p. 70).

The struggle with *having* as a way of *being* is an old one, intrinsically linked with social tensions, between the haves and have-nots, in a psychic experience of a zero sum game: making money is an aggressive act, as it involves taking it from someone else. As Borneman (1976) explains, its aetiology is based in the oral level, defined by biting, "where sadistic component instincts always combine with the desire for incorporation" (p. 31).

Yet, as Wiseman (1974) shows, it is "often only by spending it that it is possible to obtain a sense of *having* the money" (p. 53). This is akin to the subtle transformation that Bion (1962) spells out in his theory on thinking, where the absence of the object makes it possible for the thought about its presence to emerge. Also, as Chapter Six shows, Lacan can help us understand how, in the case of money, loss is inscribed in its very possession.

The theme of presence and absence is central to the story by Borges in this chapter, where a mysterious coin appears at the point where a loved one is lost. Likewise, it feels as if love itself can only begin to manifest at the point of loss. With its quasi-magical power, the unavoidable coin "expresses the object libido he did not receive as a child and therefore cannot bestow as an adult" (Borneman, 1976, p. 41).

Interestingly, the inscription on the coin—a symbolic "2" scratched on rather aggressively—is a powerful summary of money's ability to bypass the "three" and eternally seek to re-establish an elusive pairing that survives in its pure form at the level of desire alone.

To maintain its nature, money has to keep moving—it is from this that it derives its character, and it is this force that both compels and terrifies the narrator of the following story.

References

Akhtar, S. (2009). *Turning Points in Dynamic Psychotherapy: Initial Assessment, Boundaries, Money, Disruptions and Suicidal Crises*. London: Karnac.

Bion, W. R. (1962). A theory of thinking. *International Journal of Psychoanalysis*, 43: 306–310.

Borneman, E. (1976). *The Psychoanalysis of Money*. New York: Urizen Books.

Klein, M. (1935). A contribution to the psychogenesis of manic-depressive states. *International Journal of Psychoanalysis*, 16:145–174.

Wiseman, T. (1974). *The Money Motive: A Study of an Obsession*. London: Hutchinson.

Borges (1949): The Zahir*

I n Buenos Aires the Zahir is a common twenty-centavo coin into which a razor or letter opener has scratched the letters N T and the number 2; the date stamped on the face is 1929. (In Gujarat, at the end of the eighteenth century, the Zahir was a tiger; in Java it was a blind man in the Surakarta mosque, stoned by the faithful; in Persia, an astrolabe that Nadir Shah ordered thrown into the sea; in the prisons of Mahdi, in 1892, a small sailor's compass, wrapped in a shred of cloth from a turban, that Rudolf Karl von Slatin touched; in the synagogue in Córdoba, according to Zotenberg, a vein in the marble of one of the twelve hundred pillars; in the ghetto of Tetuán, the bottom of a well.) Today is the thirteenth of November; last June 7, at dawn, the Zahir came into my hands; I am not the man I was then, but I am still able to recall, and perhaps recount, what happened. I am still, albeit only partially, Borges.

On June 6, Teodelina Villar died. Back in 1930, photographs of her had littered the pages of worldly magazines; that ubiquity may have had something to do with the fact that she was thought to be a very

---

* Borges, J. L. (1949. The Zahir, in Borges, J. L. (2000). *The Aleph*. London: Penguin.

pretty woman, although that supposition was not unconditionally supported by every image of her. But no matter—Teodelina Villar was less concerned with beauty than with perfection. The Jews and Chinese codified every human situation: the *Mishnah* tells us that beginning at sunset on the Sabbath, a tailor may not go into the street carrying a needle; the Book of Rites informs us that a guest receiving his first glass of wine must assume a grave demeanour; receiving the second, a respectful, happy air. The discipline that Teodelina Villar imposed upon herself was analogous, though even more painstaking and detailed. Like Talmudists and Confucians, she sought to make every action irreproachably correct, but her task was even more admirable and difficult than theirs, for the laws of her creed were not eternal, but sensitive to the whims of Paris and Hollywood. Teodelina Villar would make her entrances into orthodox places, at the orthodox hour, with orthodox adornments, and with orthodox world-weariness but the world-weariness, the adornments, the hour, and the places would almost immediately pass out of fashion, and so come to serve (upon the lips of Teodelina Villar) for the very epitome of "tackiness". She sought the absolute, like Flaubert, but the absolute in the ephemeral. Her life was exemplary, and yet an inner desperation constantly gnawed at her. She passed through endless metamorphoses, as though fleeing from herself; her coiffure and the colour of her hair were famously unstable, as were her smile, her skin, and the slant of her eyes. From 1932 on, she was studiedly thin . . . The war gave her a great deal to think about. With Paris occupied by the Germans, how was one to follow fashion? A foreign man she has always had her doubts about was allowed to take advantage of her good will by selling her a number of stovepipe-shaped *chapeaux*. Within a year, it was revealed that those horrors *had never been worn in Paris*, and therefore were not *hats*, but arbitrary and unauthorised *caprices*. And it never rains but it pours: Dr Villar had to move to Calle Aráoz and his daughter's image began to grace advertisements for face creams and automobiles—face creams she never used and automobiles she could no longer afford! Teodelina knew that the proper exercise of her art required a great fortune; she opted to retreat rather than surrender. And besides—it pained her to compete with mere insubstantial *girls*. The sinister apartment on Aráoz, however, was too much to bear; on June 6, Teodelina Villar committed the breach of decorum of dying in the middle of Barrio Sur. Shall I confess that, moved by the sincerest of Argentine passions—snobbery—I was in love with her, and that her death actually brought tears to my eyes? Perhaps the reader has already suspected that.

At wakes, the progress of corruption allows the dead person's body to recover its former faces. At some point in the confused night of June 6, Teodelina Villar magically became what she had been twenty years before; her features recovered the authority that arrogance, money, youth, the awareness of being the *crème de la crème*, restrictions, a lack of imagination, and stolidity can give. My thoughts were more or less these: no version of that face that has so disturbed me shall ever be as memorable as this one; really, since it could almost be the first, it ought to be the last. I left her lying stiff among the flowers, her contempt for the world growing every moment more perfect in death. It was about two o'clock, I would guess, when I stepped into the street. Outside, the predictable ranks of one- and two-storey houses had taken on that abstract air they often have at night, when they are simplified by darkness and silence. Drunk with an almost impersonal pity, I wandered through the streets. On the corner of Chile and Tacuarí I spotted an open bar-and-general-store. In that establishment, to my misfortune, three men were playing *truco*.

In the rhetorical figure known as *oxymoron*, the adjective applied to a noun seems to contradict that noun. Thus, gnostics spoke of a "dark light" and alchemists, of a "black sun". Departing from my last visit to Teodelina Villar and drinking a glass of harsh brandy in a corner bar-and-grocery-store was a kind of oxymoron: the very vulgarity and facileness of it were what tempted me. (The fact that men were playing cards in the place increased the contrast.) I asked the owner for a brandy and orange juice; among my change I was given the Zahir; I looked at it for an instant, then walked outside into the street, perhaps with the beginnings of a fever. The thought struck me that there is no coin that is not the symbol of all the coins that shine endlessly down throughout history and fable. I thought of Charon's obolus; the alms that Belisarius went about begging for; Judas's thirty pieces of silver; the drachmas of the courtesan Laïs; the ancient coin proffered by one of the Ephesian sleepers; the bright coins of the wizard in the *1001 Nights*, which turned into discs of paper; Isaac Laquedem's inexhaustible denarius; the sixty thousand coins, one for every line of an epic, which Firdusi returned to a king because they were silver and

not gold; the gold doubloon nailed by Ahab to the mast; Leopold
Bloom's unreturning florin; the gold louis that betrayed the fleeing
Louis XVI near Varennes. As though in a dream, the thought that in
any coin one may read those famous connotations seemed to me of
vast, inexplicable importance. I wandered, with increasingly rapid
steps, through the deserted streets and plazas. Weariness halted me at
a corner. My eyes came to rest on a woebegone wrought-iron fence;
behind it I saw the black-and-white tiles of the porch of La Con-
cepción. I had wandered in a circle; I was just one block from the
corner where I'd been given the Zahir.

I turned the corner; the chamfered curb in darkness at the far end
of the street showed me that the establishment had closed. On
Belgrano I took a cab. Possessed, without a trace of sleepiness, almost
happy, I reflected that there is nothing less material than money, since
any coin (a twenty centavo piece, for instance) is, in all truth, a pano-
ply of all possible futures. *Money is abstract*, I said over and over, *money
is future time*. It can be an evening just outside the city, or a Brahms
melody, or maps, or chess, or coffee, or the words of Epictetus, which
teach contempt of gold; it is a Proteus more changeable than the
Proteus of the Isle of Pharos. It is unforeseeable time, Bergsonian time,
not the hard, solid time of Islam or the Porch. Adherents of determin-
ism deny that there is any event in the world that is *possible*, i.e. that
might occur; a coin symbolises our free will. (I had no suspicion at the
time that these "thoughts" were an artifice against the Zahir
and a first manifestation of its demoniac influence.) After long and
pertinacious musings, I at last fell asleep, but I dreamed that I was a
pile of coins guarded by a gryphon.

The next day I decided I'd been drunk. I also decided to free
myself of the coin that was affecting me so distressingly. I looked at
it—there was nothing particularly distinctive about it, except those
scratches. Burying it in the garden or hiding it in a corner of the library
would have been the best thing to do, but I wanted to escape its orbit
altogether, and so preferred to "lose" it. I went neither to the Basílica
del Pilar that morning nor to the cemetery; I took a subway to Constitución Station and from Constitución to San Juan and Boedo. On an
impulse, I got off at Urquiza; I walked toward the west and south; I
turned left and right, with studied randomness, at several corners,
and on a street that looked to me like all the others I went into the first
tavern I came to, ordered a brandy, and paid with the Zahir. I half

closed my eyes, even behind the dark lenses of my spectacles, and managed not to see the numbers on the houses or the name of the street. That night, I took a sleeping draft and slept soundly.

Until the end of June I distracted myself by composing a tale of fantasy. The tale contains two or three enigmatic circumlocutions—*sword-water* instead of *blood*, for example, and *dragon's-bed* for *gold*—and is written in the first person. The narrator is an ascetic who has renounced all commerce with mankind and lives on a kind of moor. (The name of the place is Gnitaheidr.) Because of the simplicity and innocence of his life, he is judged by some to be an angel; that is a charitable sort of exaggeration, because no one is free of sin—he himself (to take the example nearest at hand) has cut his father's throat, though it is true that his father was a famous wizard who had used his magic to usurp an infinite treasure to himself. Protecting this treasure from cankerous human greed is the mission to which the narrator has devoted his life; day and night he stands guard over it. Soon, perhaps too soon, that watchfulness will come to an end: the stars have told him that the sword that will sever it forever has already been forged. (The name of the sword is Gram.) In an increasingly tortured style, the narrator praises the lustrousness and flexibility of his body; one paragraph offhandedly mentions "scales"; another says that the treasure he watches over is of red rings and gleaming gold. At the end, we realise that the ascetic is the serpent Fafnir and the treasure on which the creature lies coiled is the gold of the Nibelungen. The appearance of Sigurd abruptly ends the story.

I have said that composing that piece of trivial nonsense (in the course of which I interpolated, with pseudoerudition, a line or two from the *Fafnismal*) enabled me to put the coin out of my mind. There were nights when I was so certain I'd be able to forget it that I would wilfully remember it. The truth is, I abused those moments; starting to recall turned out to be much easier than stopping. It was futile to tell myself that that abominable nickel disk was no different from the infinite other identical, inoffensive disks that pass from hand to hand every day. Moved by that reflection, I attempted to think about another coin, but I couldn't. I also recall another (frustrated) experiment that I performed with Chilean five- and ten-centavo pieces and a Uruguayan two-centavo piece. On July 16, I acquired a pound sterling; I didn't look at it all that day, but that night (and others) I placed it under a magnifying glass and studied it in the light of a powerful electric lamp.

Then I made a rubbing of it. The rays of light and the dragon and St George availed me naught; I could not rid myself of my *idée fixe*.

In August, I decided to consult a psychiatrist. I did not confide the entire absurd story to him; I told him I was tormented by insomnia and that often I could not free my mind of the image of an object, any random object—a coin, say . . . A short time later, in a bookshop on Calle Sarmiento, I exhumed a copy of Julius Barlach's *Urkunden zur Geschichte der Zahirsage* (Breslau, 1899).

Between the covers of that book was a description of my illness. The introduction said that the author proposed to "gather into a single manageable octavo volume every existing document that bears upon the superstition of the Zahir, including four articles held in the Habicht archives and the original manuscript of Philip Meadows Taylor's report on the subject". Belief in the Zahir is of Islamic ancestry, and dates, apparently, to some time in the eighteenth century. (Barlach impugns the passages that Zotenberg attributes to Abul-Feddah.) In Arabic, "*zahir*" means visible, manifest, evident; in that sense, it is one of the ninety-nine names of God; in Muslim countries, the masses use the word for "beings or things which have the terrible power to be unforgettable, and whose image eventually drives people mad". Its first undisputed witness was the Persian polymath and dervish Lutf Ali Azur; in the corroborative pages of the biographical encyclopaedia titled *Temple of Fire*, Ali Azur relates that in a certain school in Shiraz there was a copper astrolabe "constructed in such a way that any man who looked upon it once could think of nothing else, so that the king commanded that it be thrown into the deepest depths of the sea, in order that men might not forget the universe". Meadows Taylor's account is somewhat more extensive; the author served the Nazim of Hyderabad, and composed the famous novel *Confessions of a Thug*. In 1832, on the outskirts of Bhuj, Taylor heard the following uncommon expression used to signify madness or saintliness: "Verily he has looked upon the tiger". He was told that the reference was to a magic tiger that was the perdition of all who saw it, even from a great distance, for never afterward could a person stop thinking about it. Someone mentioned that one of those stricken people had fled to Mysore, where he had painted the figure of the tiger in a palace. Years later, Taylor visited the prisons of that district; in the jail at Nighur, the governor showed him a cell whose floor, walls and vaulted ceiling were covered by a drawing (in barbaric colours that time, before obliterating had refined) of an infinite tiger. It was a tiger composed of many tigers, in the most dizzying of ways; it was crisscrossed with tigers, striped with tigers and contained seas and Himalayas and armies that resembled other tigers. The painter, a fakir, had died many years before, in that same cell; he had come from Sind or perhaps Gujarat and his initial purpose had been to draw a map of the world. Of that purpose there remained some vestiges within the monstrous image. Taylor told this story to Muhammad al-Yemeni, of Fort William; al-Yemeni said that there was no creature in the world that did not tend toward becoming a *Zaheer*[1], but that the All-Merciful does not allow two things to be a *Zaheer* at the same time, since a single one is capable of entrancing multitudes. He said that there is always a Zahir—in the Age of Ignorance it was the idol called Yahuk, and then a prophet from Khorasan who wore a veil spangled with precious stones or a mask of gold.[2] He also noted that Allah was inscrutable.

Over and over I read Barlach's monograph. I cannot sort out my emotions; I recall my desperation when I realised that nothing could any longer save me, the inward relief of knowing that I was not to blame for my misfortune, the envy I felt for those whose Zahir was not a coin but a slab of marble or a tiger. How easy it is not to think of a tiger!, I recall thinking. I also recall the remarkable uneasiness I felt when I read this paragraph: "One commentator of the *Gulshan i Raz* states that 'he who has seen the Zahir soon shall see the Rose'" and quotes a line of poetry interpolated into Attar's *Asrar Nama* ("The Book of Things Unknown"): "the Zahir is the shadow of the Rose and the rending of the Veil".

On the night of Teodelina's wake, I had been surprised not to see among those present Sra. Abascal, her younger sister. In October, I ran into a friend of hers.

"Poor Julita," the woman said to me, "she's became so odd. She's been put into Bosch. How she must be crushed by those nurses spoon-feeding her! She's still going on and on about that coin, just like Morena Sackmann's chauffeur."

Time, which softens recollections, only makes the memory of the Zahir all the sharper. First I could see the face of it, then the reverse; now I can see both sides at once. It is not as though the Zahir were made of glass, since one side is not superimposed upon the other—rather, it is as though the vision were itself spherical, with the Zahir rampant in the centre. Anything that is not the Zahir comes to me as though through a filter, and from a distance Teodelina's disdainful image, physical pain. Tennyson said that if we could but understand a single flower we might know who we are and what the world is. Perhaps he was trying to say that there is nothing, however humble, that does not imply the history of the world and its infinite concatenation of causes and effects. Perhaps he was trying to say that the visible world can be seen entire in every image, just as Schopenhauer tells us that the Will expresses itself entire in every man and woman. The Kabbalists believed that man is a microcosm, a symbolic mirror of the universe; if one were to believe Tennyson, *everything* would be—*everything*, even the unbearable Zahir.

Before the year 1948, Julia's fate will have overtaken me. I will have to be fed and dressed, I will not know whether it's morning or night, I will not know who the man Borges was. Calling that future terrible is a fallacy, since none of the future's circumstances will in any way affect me. One might as well call "terrible" the pain of an anaesthetised patient whose skull is being trepanned. I will no longer perceive the universe, I will perceive the Zahir. Idealist doctrine has it that the verbs "to live" and "to dream" are at every point synonymous; for me, thousands of appearances will pass into one; a complex dream will pass into a simple one. Others will dream that I am mad, while I dream of the Zahir. When every person on earth thinks, day and night, of the Zahir, which will be dream and which reality, the earth or the Zahir?

In the waste and empty hours of the night I am still able to walk through the streets. Dawn often surprises me upon a bench in the Plaza Garay, thinking (or trying to think) about that passage in the *Asrar Nama* where it is said that the Zahir is the shadow of the Rose and the rending of the Veil. I link that pronouncement to this fact: in order to lose themselves in God, the Sufis repeat their own name or the ninety-nine names of God until the names mean nothing any more. I long to travel that path. Perhaps by thinking about the Zahir unceasingly, I can manage to wear it away; perhaps behind the coin is God.

For Wally Zenner

Notes

1.   This is Taylor's spelling of the word.

2.   Barlach observes that Yahuk figures in the Qur'ān (71:23) and that the prophet is Al-Moqanna (the Veiled Prophet) and that no one, with the exception of the surprising correspondent Philip Meadows Taylor, has ever linked those two figures to the Zahir.

CHAPTER SIX

Money and desire: a Lacanian perspective

Anca Carrington

Introduction

A different and most revealing approach to understanding the social dimension of money is made possible by the Lacanian insight into the registers of human experience as structured by three orders: the Imaginary, the Real,[1] and the Symbolic. In this case, the notion of Symbolic is transformed from the status of adjective to that of noun, denoting the world of language and the law[1] governing human interactions. Most importantly, the Symbolic thus understood is "the realm of the Law which regulates desire in the Oedipus complex" (Evans, 1996, p. 202), characterised as it is by triadic structures, where any intersubjective relationship is mediated by a third term, the Other. Also, this is the realm of absence and lack (Evans, 1996). In particular, for Lacan, the Oedipus complex is "the paradigmatic triangular structure" (Evans, 1996, p. 127) in which the key role belongs to the father as the third term that turns the dyadic relationship between mother and child into a triadic one. The Father is the one who brings in the Law and makes possible the move into the symbolic realm.

The relevance of this approach to an enriched comprehension of money is great, as the Lacanian understanding of communication itself, the exchange of words, is as the most basic form of exchange—something that money also accomplishes by design. That is to say, both money and words function as currency in the domain and under the force of symbolism. The symbolic dimension of language is defined by the signifier, which stands for anything "that is inscribed in a system in which it takes on value purely by difference from the other elements in the system" (Evans, 1996, p. 187). This can be, indeed, *anything*—a word, but also an object, a relationship, an act—whose meaning is not intrinsic, but defined by its relative position. Among these, Lacan identifies money as "the most annihilating signifier there is of all signification" (*"signifiant le plus annihilant qui soit the de toute signification"*—Lacan, 1966, p. 37), or what Fink (1997), a leading Lacanian scholar, calls "the great leveller or equaliser" (p. 265). This particular link between money and language gives a fresh meaning to the common statement "money talks". Like the father in early life, and then like language, money occupies a powerful and provocative, but much needed, third position.

Understood as a signifier, money makes an ideal candidate for the position of *agalma* carrier, a holder of little intrinsic value that holds within a most precious offering (Bailly, 2009, p. 131), the object of desire. And because unconscious desire constitutes the driving force of life, and, thus, according to Lacan, the essence of human existence (Evans, 1996, p. 36), its quality is more that of a condition than that of affect. Not easily articulated in words, desire organises itself around imaginary objects, which fulfil a psychological need rather than a physical one, that is to say, objects that can support a fantasy (Bailly, 2009, p. 129). As we have already seen, money is well established as exactly such an entity.

Traced back to its origins, the ultimate object of desire for the child is that which the mother seeks when she is away, that which the child must lack for her to be pursuing it elsewhere—what Lacan calls the Phallus, the desire of the Other (the mother, to start with). This is also what the (m)other lacks, or else would not be seeking it. This is the object that the child, in fantasy, seeks to become, as a way of emerging into that which can satisfy mother's desire, the desirable and desired one. A triangular configuration is made possible through the assertion of the presence of the Father as symbolic function, rather than actual person. He functions as a barrier to unbridled desire and representative of the Law, forcing the pursuit of satisfaction away from the mother, with money a powerful candidate for carrying it, in its capacity to maintain a link with a lost object, while also marking a separation from it. What is central to this match is money's ability to function as an unconscious equivalent of any object invested with desire, that is to say, to act as an agalma. Lacan (2013) defines this as "the object the subject believes his desire aims at and regarding which he most completely mistakes the object for the cause of desire" (p. 70).

It is on this particular aspect that the paper below concentrates, as it explores the functioning of money as a signifier and its place in the social domain, where it both succeeds in navigating the constraints on desire, and fails at it—so that we all return to money and the promise it carries, time and again, both individually and collectively.

Gilles Arnaud shows the ways in which money is used to neutralise the symbolic debt of castration—that which we all have to give up in order to separate and become individual subjects—and explores its ability to preserve our phantasy of omnipotence in its power to deny difference, while ultimately remaining a sign of pure absence, with its power to provide the illusion of representing, or even replacing, the lost and prohibited mother and all that she represents.

Note

1. The Imaginary relates to the experiences in the domain of image, of how the body is seen, while the Real captures the libidinal life of the body.

References

Bailly, L. (2009). *Lacan: A Beginner's Guide*. Oxford: Oneworld.

Evans, D. (1996). *An Introductory Dictionary of Lacanian Psychoanalysis*. London: Routledge.

Fink, B. (1997). *A Clinical Introduction to Lacanian Psychoanalysis: Theory and Technique*. London: Harvard University Press.

Lacan, J. (1966). Le séminaire sur "La Lettre Volée". In: *Ecrits I* (pp. 11–61). Paris: Le Seuil.

Lacan, J. (2013). *On the Names-of-the-Father*. Cambridge: Polity Press.

Arnaud (2003): Money as signifier: A Lacanian insight into the monetary order*

"So saying, he pulled out of his pocket a small coin, which he flung on to the table. 'Just hear how true it rings. Almost the same sound as the real one. One would swear it was gold. I was taken in by it this morning, just as the grocer who passed it on to me had been taken in himself, he told me. It isn't quite the same weight, I think; but it has the brightness and the sound of a real piece; it is coated with gold, so that, all the same, it is worth a little more than two sous; but it's made of glass. It'll wear transparent'." (Gide, 1931)

A two-sided currency

Money has rarely been considered as worthy of study by psychologists, perhaps because it seems to be a matter first and foremost for economists and financiers (Furnham & Argyle, 1998). The small number of (mostly psychoanalytically-oriented) clinicians who have dealt directly with the subject have

* Originally published in *Free Associations*, 10(1): 25–34.

usually confined their investigations to the importance that pecuniary questions are capable of taking on in neurotic processes (Fenichel, 1947; Borneman, 1978; Goldberg & Lewis, 1978; Matthews, 1991; Reiss-Schimmel, 1993) or, correlatively, psychoanalytical treatments, where not only payment as such but also the specific form it takes are considered to be part of the analysis' framework. According to this principle then, "hard cash" is particularly apt to serve as an object of transference (Collège de psychanalystes, 1986, 1988).

For my part, as an organizational consultant influenced by analytical thought, I would like to go beyond the clinical and psychopathological perspective and try to use psychoanalytic theory, especially the Lacanian conception of the Symbolic, to throw light on money's social dimension. In particular, I shall attempt to show that phenomena, such as inflation, stock market crises, counterfeiting or the dematerialization of means of payment, that affect the role and place of currency in human interactions do not threaten our cultural system in the same way. In fact, these various structural or conjunctural phenomena weaken (to a greater or lesser degree, depending on the case) two quite distinct levels of money's symbolic function: namely, money's functioning as a sign and its functioning as a signifier. Although it is far more common for the first of these two signifying functions to be singled out in the case of money, it seems to me, for reasons that I shall go on to elaborate in the pages that follow, that the second function – money as signifier – might well prove to be more crucial for human beings from a societal, or even anthropological, standpoint (Sagna, 2001).

Money for psychoanalysis: Symbolic permutations and anal eroticism

An apt starting-point for a psychoanalytical reflection on money might well be found in an early observation of Freud himself, who was to declare to Fliess in a letter dated 16 January 1898, that "money did not form the object of an infantile wish"[1] – which is why, as the well-known saying puts it, money proves incapable of "making one happy" as an adult. Yet, it can nevertheless give the impression of doing so, to the extent that it is capable – as we know from Freudian metapsychology – of functioning as the unconscious substitute and equivalent for any "object" whatsoever that is invested by the libido of the subject, be this oral, phallic or, especially, anal (Borneman, 1978).

Indeed, it is because infants view their faeces as the first tangible proof of their capacity to produce something meaningful, on both a material level and a "relational" one, that money stands in a relation of symbolic equivalence, for the unconscious of every subject, with the notions of faeces, gift, penis, and baby (Freud, 1905, 1908, 1917).

On a material level, faeces represent for children their first possessions of value. Indeed, if children tend at first, roughly between the ages of two and three, to take an auto-erotic pleasure in defecating (the first phase of the anal stage), they subsequently discover, around the age of three or four, that they can obtain a more intense excitation by holding back their stool (the second phase of the anal stage). This is the source of the pleasure adults take in holding onto money, valuable objects or, yet again, time (as shown by the character-traits of avarice and parsimony, as well as the pleasure of hoarding or saving), in accordance with the equation of money and excrement.

As regards the relational point of view, it is not long before the child comes up against a parental injunction – usually expressed by the mother – to "do" when and where it is necessary. The child thus finds himself or herself faced with an alternative: either to obey and defecate in the pot upon which he or she is placed, and thereby secure maternal satisfaction, along with rewards and caresses; or to disobey, in a show of defiance directed at the beloved mother, by "doing" anytime and anywhere (in bed, for example) or by refusing to perform when asked to, and thereby annoy, or even anger, his or her mother.

The first option consists in the child's presenting his or her first real gift to the mother – namely, the gift of his or her stools, capable of extracting cries of joy or surprise from the latter – and in thereby taking up an attitude of object love. The second option amounts to the child's preferring a narcissistic position – refusal, stubbornness, obstinacy, opposition, etc. – and his or her obtaining an aggressive satisfaction (the anal sadistic aspect of which Freud speaks). This would form the source of the pleasure that adults can take in refusing demands made by other people – such as demands for a pay rise made by employees in a firm, with such a refusal being all the more significant, on the symbolic level, when the rise in question is almost negligible in strictly financial terms.

In the most extreme case, according to the psychoanalytical argument that is often put forward, an overly active or precocious repression of the child's psychosexual development during the anal stage – especially at the moment of toilet training – can lead to the development, in later life, of a veritable obsessional (or, as it was sometimes called, anal) neurosis. Since the pathbreaking work of Oskar Pfister on the psychical structure of classical capitalism and the financial mind (Borneman, 1978), an entire current of thought (Reich, Fromm, etc.) has endeavoured to locate within the capitalist system the indices of a collective obsessional neurotic syndrome. Just as the child is under the illusion of the omnipotence of his or her excrements, so the capitalist would tend to believe that his or her money gives him or her the power – and, above all, the right – to do whatever he or she so desires. This is all the more the case given that "globalization" seems to increase multinational corporations' power of influence (which rivals that of nation states) and that capitalism now has a free rein almost everywhere in the world (with the notable exception of Cuba and North Korea).

Yet, as Reiss-Schimmel has remarked (1993), it is time to free ourselves from Freud's overly exclusive association of money and anality. Or, at least, it would appear necessary to distance oneself from the caricature that has often been presented of this association and which "has contributed to maintaining a certain misunderstanding between psychoanalysis and economic science" (Vallet, 1996, p. 688). Moreover, certain post-Freudian theories (Abraham, Ferenczi, Jones), which were endorsed at the time by the father of psychoanalysis himself, already insist on the fact that only the retentional and accumulative aspect of money is, strictly speaking, related to the anal character. These theories notably put forward the hypothesis that money's appropriative and incorporative aspect would, for its part, belong to the first phase of the oral stage.

Correlatively, Martin (1984) has pointed out that, while analytical theory has shown money to figure amongst the symptoms of obsessional neurosis in a very precise way, the same cannot be said with respect to other neurotic structures and positions or the perversions and psychoses – a shortcoming that his own research attempts to redress, however slightly. Moreover, Martin does not stop there but considers that any attribution of money's signifying effects to some psychogenetic stage or other is in itself inadequate, particularly if one wants to succeed in defining what it is that makes money such an eminent symbolic component of our societies.

Indeed, as Schimmel once again points out:

> while the position that money has in the symbolic chain 'faeces (gift-money)/penis/baby' makes of it a continuation of the anal erotic drive from which it stems, the drive component that cathects it undergoes extremely unusual vicissitudes. As heir to the gift, money is stripped of all narcissistic value in keeping with the exclusively object-related dimension in which it is situated, and yet it is equally disconnected from objects cathected by the genital drive: it seems, therefore, to be a desexualized partial object that is destined uniquely to serve as a means of exchange. (Schimmel, 1990, p. 536)

Money and the field of the sign

In its primary – let's say, economic or financial – application, money is an instrument both for conducting transactions and for measuring. This means that, without any judgement as to the intrinsic 'usefulness' of its material composition,[2] money is called upon to fulfil a symbolic function as sign, insofar as it does indeed (in conformity with Peirce's definition) signify something for someone – such as the "other" of a trade relation, a paid job, or stock market operation. Furthermore, it is a sign stamped with a dual aspect as it were, since it is not only the sign of any and all merchandise as well as of exchange itself (Schimmel, 1990), but also, undoubtedly in a more abstract way, the sign of wealth and value as such.

Indeed, for economists, money represents first of all that general equivalent of commodities which Marx was to analyze [sic] in all its details.[3] Or, more precisely, it operates economically as the general equivalent of the exchange value of commodities in the work-production relation. With the transformation of things into commodities, money appears essentially, therefore, to be the sign of any object, and even the sign of surplus value or assets.

In addition, the exchange value of commodities is materialized in the form of prices, understood as measures of one quantity in relation to another, considered as conventional units. This is why money, as the quotient and relation between things (including human labour and wages, or companies as global entities and the stock market rate) allows not only the posting of differences, but also the opening up of a space of communication and mutual understanding with others (which is a propriety of the sign). As such, it is well and truly a vector of the social bond (Clerc, 2000).

As the support of this economic function, money functions concomitantly, in its more specifically financial application, as the sign of the matter of which it is made: namely, the metal of which it is composed or, more precisely, the stamped paper which takes the latter's place. This makes it the preferred sign of wealth and value as such.[4] The signified of such a sign is, therefore, no longer commodities, labour or shares (the latter being, themselves, other signs) as such, but rather, for instance, the equivalent value in gold that serves to justify and legitimate the existence of "representative" bank notes.[5] The main difference, on the symbolic level, between these two types of money's functioning as sign lies no doubt in the fact that money as "sign of all commodities" refers to an open system comprising an infinite number of objects, present or future, while money as "sign of the matter of which it is made" implicitly refers to a closed system of gold securities (or other securities) that are theoretically retained in the possession of nation-states as the guarantee of their currency (Arnaud & Louart, 2000).

Yet I would underline that this reference to securities is, indeed, 'implicit', for, in reality – as has already been briefly indicated – stamped paper is fundamentally the sign of a conventional value, and this is all more the case since currencies have been declared inconvertible into gold. In fact, bank notes (which are so aptly named "*coupures*" – literally, "cuttings" or "clippings" – in French) are seen as fragments of what one imagines as a finite whole, namely the supply of paper money authorized for circulation ('legal currency') at the level both of a national currency and the European or international monetary system, where conversions are governed by official exchange rates that again open up a transactional space.

That said, we are now in a position to examine briefly certain disturbances that affect the monetary machine and to indicate, where relevant, what dangers such disturbances might hold for our society, according to the way in which they perturb the sign function.

Let us start by examining a number of ways in which the sign function can be distorted by individuals themselves. For example, some people behave as though money need not signify the absence of the represented object. That being the case, when they handle money, they identify themselves with the very fact of having money in their possession and, in this way, neutralize – by avoiding the question of desire, since the latter is embodied by the money-object – the symbolic debt of castration. Martin has, moreover, very cleverly shown by playing on the homophony between *denier* (i.e., the eighteenth century coin) and *dénier* (the French for "deny") that money as the sign of exchange, insofar as it allows the subject (of the statement) to treat any object or quality as equivalent to any other, is at the same time what denies that the aforesaid subject is relegated to an empty space in his or her relation with what Lacan names the object "small a" – the fundamental object of desire – represented by the objects or commodities in question. In this way, money preserves for the Ego its phantasm of omnipotence, since it is power to act. The miser's act of hoarding can be construed, from this point of view, as primarily aiming to restore to the monetary symbol its value as object, even to the point of fetishizing it. That this is the case seems all the more plausible given that the exponential development of 'hypermoney' (payment by bank cards, automatic credit transfers, dummy entries, electronic payments on the internet, etc.) tends to "euphemize" the material reality of monetary exchange (Guillaume, 1992). As a result, money would, in our modern societies, even tend to become an end in itself: a "holy fetish", as Enriquez (1999) puts it.

On the other hand, there are people who end up singlemindedly chasing after money not because they overrate its material consistency, but – on the contrary – because they overvalue its function as sign, promoting this, as Simmel foresaw a century ago, to the level of an all-powerful symbol by means of which they can envisage buying anything they want, even if this means spending what they do not have, as with consumer credit (Gardaz, 1997). Indeed, as such an all-powerful symbol, money seems to function as the "measure" of all things, with every aspect of social reality, however large or small, finding itself weighed up in terms of its profitability – including "human assets" in the workplace (Le Mouël, 1991). One could well wonder, for that matter, whether a phantasm of mastery of this kind might not form the backdrop for the notion as such of a "single currency". Be this as it may, however, such a purely monetary approach has the effect of blinding one to the important economic tendency that seeks to obtain ever more use – value for less money – which is why it makes at least as much sense to increase use-capacity as it does to increase buying power.

Finally, other people "reverse" the signifying relation to such a degree that money becomes the signified of the objects of which it is supposedly the sign, as is the case when these objects' use value is completely hidden by their exchange value. From then on, money, which can replace all and anything (commodities, etc.) insofar as it "perpetually defers the difference between things" (Martin, 1984, p. 34), tends no longer to represent anything other than itself, while goods or assets – ever-elusive as such – are characterized uniquely by their capacity to be converted into cash.[6] It is for this reason that money can operate "solo" in the present economy, without any other organizational logic than its own; but the risk of such a mode of functioning is that 'the expansion of market relations will create a world without rules, without morality and without justice' (Boltanski & Thévenot, 1991, p. 348). "Mad money" then, indeed: this expression popularized by Alain Minc (1990)[7] would, in fact, seem particularly apt – at least, if one agrees that a functioning freed from any external law does indeed qualify as madness.

Having shown how the sign function can be modified by individuals, let us now examine in what way and to what degree certain conjunctural disturbances affecting the financial sphere can also place money's sign function in difficulty. Take the example of a change-over of currency, which is a particularly topical subject given the recent putting into circulation of the euro in place of some twelve national European currencies. What is involved here is a modification of the monetary convention, which, although it can certainly cause many users a great deal of confusion,[8] does not, however, damage money's sign function as such. For those countries forming part of what is now fitting to call "Euroland", the transition to a single currency tends rather to clarify this function, not only by homogenizing trade (allowing an easier calculation and a better comparison of prices), but also by doing away with exchange operations (thus solving problems of convertibility and creating a common language across frontiers).

On the other hand, it is a very different situation when it is a matter of devaluations and other inflationary crises. What is involved here is, either, a relatively important and rapid deterioration of the monetary convention linking a currency to a standard of reference or to other currencies, such that the currency in question loses value (devaluation), or an excessive printing of money, leading to an inordinate amount of currency being injected into the economic cycle and a resulting increase in demand and rise in prices (inflation).[9] Unlike the change-over of a currency, such financial disorders (or disasters) can only weaken the "sign" aspect of money. Exactly to what extent they do so will depend on the circumstances.

In a context of devaluation or inflation, it does indeed become more and more difficult for the legal tender "to designate". For the currency to remain valid as a means of exchange, it is necessary to "add more of it", at the risk of lowering, or indeed shaking, public confidence in the representative function of paper-money as such. When the rate of the rouble fell some eighty percent [sic] in the space of just a few weeks in 1998, due in particular to the shock wave of the Asian crisis, there was, for example, a return to bartering as the standard means of transaction in most of the Russian provinces. Yet, this degeneration of the currency's sign function did not simply render commercial relations precarious. Its consequences ranged from political improprieties that were observed at the very highest level of the State to people behaving in ways that threatened not only public order, but indeed national and international security – as when employees in nuclear centres who were without pay cried out for all to hear that, if they were not paid soon, they would accept no responsibility for what might happen. Such repercussions as these adequately testify to the scrambling of symbolic reference points at work in Russian society as a whole.

Function and field of the signifier in the monetary order

Beyond this function as sign, money also entails a function as signifier. This is the principle set out by Lacan himself in his famous *Seminar on The Purloined Letter* (1966), when he speaks of "the most annihilating signifier there is of all signification, namely money" (p. 37). Taking up the concept of the signifier in its Lacanian acceptation, Martin elaborates this innovatory position as meaning that "money is a signifier without signification" (p. 15). Following this perspective, we might point out that the vocation of the signifier is indeed to refer uniquely to its own repetition, which means, in other words, that there is no equivalent in the register of the signifier, there is no signified that holds.

In fact, the sign appears as functional insofar as it is used and exchanged; one knows where it is and what path it follows when it is displaced. This is the case of banknotes, which, although freely-circulating discrete parts of a money supply – as we have seen – are always referred back to the whole in accordance with an auto-regulated rate. The signifier, for its part, is devoid of functionality. It is – to put it this way – the sign of a pure absence (a pact with death, in Lacan's words). Indeed, the signifier-money is always lacking, and precisely to the extent that one possesses it since loss is inscribed in its very possession – which explains why one can never have enough of it. As a result, it is of no relevance to determine whether its nature is more anal than oral or even phallic (in the sense of some sort of psychogenesis); here, money is nothing else than the mark of the impossible identity of the subject.

There are two fundamental reasons why money can find itself promoted to the status of signifier. First, as Viderman (1992) points out, money, in its capacity as a sign, functions as a "universal exchanger" which is perpetually "drifting", without ever designating anything in particular (be it a commodity or itself). Gori and Hoffman conclude, for this reason, that:

> Money is the trait that as much establishes a link with the lost object as it marks a separation with the latter. Money is a possession that engraves the very loss it appeases – which is not simply the loss of the object whose absence it marks, but, indeed, its own loss, insofar as it is taken up in a permanent exchange continually open to negotiation and re-evaluation within the monetary flow. Unlike donation and sacrifice, or the gift with its enactment of an imaginary barter, money falls within a system that transcends all sense. Strictly speaking, money is senseless. Money is money, notwithstanding all the libidinal, subjective and intersubjective meanings from which it cannot be separated. (1999, p. 339)

That being the case, once there is an acknowledgement of money-as-signifier, it is circulation that tends to become the main notion as regards monetary matters, and no longer reciprocity or exchange (Forrester, 1998, p. 164).

The second reason why the monetary sign takes on a signifying function has to do with the fact that the conventional aspect of money-as-sign is not intrinsic to it but depends upon "public discourse" and its combination of signifiers. Put in Lacanian terms, this means that money is a power of the Other (with a capital "o") – that is, to put it schematically, Language – and not of the subject as is the case with the sign. In this way, it "becomes the very signifier of what subjectivity loses by having to show itself in and through language – or in other words, by existing only through and within the operation of fractioning, that is, of debit" (Gori & Hoffman, 1999, p. 339). It follows that the paper or metal of which money is composed borrow the laws of their exchange from language (metaphor of want-of-being, metonymy of desire, signifying materiality) and that each and every subject confronted to their exchange comes up against the law of the signifier (in the form of the absence in the Other of any signifier of the subject).

Admittedly, the comparison between money and language is hardly new, dating at least from the origin of Indo-European languages in which the words for money and argument derive from the same root (Assoun et al., 1997, p. 690). Nor is it specific to psychoanalysis; its trace can notably be found in literature, as in the texts of Mallarmé or Gide, as regards French literature for instance. But we want to carry the comparison further, by pointing out that the relation of money to wealth is both symbolic and arbitrary, in the sense that money's value, in our modern societies, is conferred not by the weight of its constitutive metal, but, on the contrary, by the societies and states that claim to guarantee the monetary system as a whole. From this point of view, the underlying stakes involved in this signifying and "securizing" function that money underpins on the symbolic level appear all the more clearly when the consistence and reliability of this function are threatened, as they are in the extreme by the existence of forged currency (David, 1994).

We have, in fact, often wondered why the production and traffic of forged bills are so actively repressed and so heavily punished – to a far greater extent, for instance, than are theft or embezzlement, even when these are perpetrated on a large scale. It seems to us now that the answer can only lie in the following principle, which is at the very base of our social order: namely, that solely the currency guaranteed by the nation-states – that is, the Symbolic, of which money is precisely a representative – ought to circulate. The very durability of our social cultural system is at stake here, for this system could be overturned or even destroyed by the proliferation of false references that are necessarily excluded from any form of legal and symbolic guarantee.

Following the example of language, money as a signifier in no way belongs to the subject who, in fact, only makes use of it. Reiss-Schimmel (1993, p. 15) remarks in this context that: "the genesis of monetary forms and functions testifies . . . to a progressive integration of the function of a third element as well as to an equally progressive reinforcement of the collective capacities of symbolization." As Parsons, Luhmann, Habermas and Giddens have each seen in their own way, this makes money well and truly a representative of the Symbolic (i.e., the register of language). Psychoanalytical theory adds to this that the consistence and reliability of such a representative are necessary to psychical functioning, in the sense that the inscription of human beings in a signifying order is what allows them to accede to Desire, no less than to the social Rule (Enriquez, 1997, p. 398). In short, individuals imperatively need the Symbolic, not so much in order to communicate with others (which is a function of the sign), but to accede to the status of subjects in relation to the Law (a function of the signifier).

The same goes for money in the case of the adult, or excrement in the case of the child, as for language: the law and value of symbolic exchange always emanate from the Other (respectively: the State, the Mother, and the Signifying Order). The individuation and separation of each subject with respect to his or her "Other, with a capital 'o'" requires, then, both a sacrifice (in the form of a payment of money according to social norms, the gift of one's stools, or a demand passing through the defiles of language) and the renunciation of a jouissance[10] (the immediate satisfaction of needs, anal retention, or acting-out).

In this respect, forged currency is a parody: it apes, as it were, real currency, and renders this ridiculous in much the same way as an ape imitating a man makes fun of the latter. And as one cannot make fun of symbolic guarantees with impunity, the proliferation of forged currency is anything but neutral: not only economic values but equally ethical and juridical values, etc., soon appear as suspicious (Goux, 1984) since currency is the expression of a global sovereignty (Aglietta & Orléan, 1998). It is therefore socially essential, or even vital, to unmask and stop counterfeiters and traffickers. In this case, forged currency is indeed a much more serious problem for the continuity of our social order than are inflationary crises, devaluations, or even the laundering of illegal drug takings, even if these phenomena are no less 'sensational'. For, while the latter constitute an attack against the symbolic function by calling into question its character as "sign", counterfeiting is alone capable of grievously harming or even destroying this function through its injection of falsity into the signifier (i.e., money-as-signifier) as such.

The principle of forged currency – especially when its fraudulent imitation of real currency is so perfect that it is almost impossible to distinguish between the two – implies then that the watermarks and other official marks used by national banks are no longer a guarantee. If we suppose there to be a certain quantity of forged currency already circulating in the twists and turns of social exchanges, we are led to the terrifying conclusion that the true bears the false within itself. This makes it clearer why states constantly strive to devise ways of rendering their currency ever more difficult to forge.

Such considerations concerning money as a signifier thus give support to the idea, as Chaskiel (2000) has mentioned, that it is impossible to completely trust the Symbolic, however absolutely indispensable this may otherwise be to Man. First, as we have just seen, it may well be the case that the true bears the false within itself, but, more generally, money is never able to pay for or replace those minute fetishes (trivia, memories, etc.) that are so dear to us and which testify, over the course of our lives, to the absence of the fundamental object of desire (the proof that one cannot buy everything). The same is true of language's signifiers, for, as Lacan has remarked, these show themselves to be inappropriate – even within an analytical treatment – for calling up the "real" of the lost and prohibited mother (which Lacan, following Freud, names the "Thing") that unconsciously constitutes the Sovereign Good. The signifying system is, in fact, marked by a hole of the "real" that, although masked, not only constitutes a structural flaw but one that moreover proves to be indispensable to the very consistence and operativity of the system as such.

A semblance of a conclusion: The wisdom of money

That said, while money does not succeed in representing, much less replacing, the Thing, it does nevertheless give the illusion of

doing so. We might then say that, beyond money's symbolic equiva-
lencies and permutations in the unconscious, there is what we would
call "seeming-money", in thinking here of Lacan's definition of "seeming" or "semblance" (le semblant). According to this definition, as
outlined by Martin, seeming is effectively: "to be and not to be what
it is, to be and not to be where it is, which is precisely what excludes
any possible confusion with the object insofar as the latter offers itself
to human industry and, thereby, to both exchange and use." (1984,
p. 21)

We are now in a better position to understand Lacan's statement
that the unconscious, as a discourse centred around the impossibility
of the object small "a", object of jouissance, may be likened to the
emergence of a certain function of the signifier within a register
governed by the principle of semblance. Yet while falling within the
register of seeming, this function that the subject is capable of assum-
ing is qualified by Lacan as a primary function of truth, in the sense
of the truth of an illusion (Dufour, 1998). The example of money thus
helps to make us aware that the universe of the symbolic is also that
of semblance and that one should not be duped by this (as forged
money, that seeming of a seeming, so exemplarily illustrates).

In short, the representation of money with what we have just seen
of its "seeming" aspect, leads us to reflect upon the Symbolic and
upon the fact that, however immensely powerful this is, it shows
itself, at the same time, to be no less fallible (Arnaud, 1999). We might
then say, by way of conclusion, that a psychoanalytic reflection on
money does not so much consist in applying the psychoanalytic
conception of the Symbolic to money, as in grasping, thanks to money,
the function of the Symbolic from a psychoanalytic point of view.

This is the case even in the day to day existence of organizations,
where a consideration of money's place, circulation and use confirms
above all the "Symbolic's hold over the real" (Lacan). We can show
this through a simple example, drawn from our recent experience. We
have, in fact, recently carried out a research action within a sector of
the public service on the feasibility of applying management methods
from the private sphere to the public sphere. Among the preliminary
questions we had to consider was that of why management in the
public sector, in distinction to the private sphere (as has often been
observed), is essentially a matter of dealing with employees'; claims
and repeated strikes.

Dissatisfied with the sociological approaches that readily single out the perverse effects of job security in these displays of social and union demands, we were to find a heuristic way of tackling the question by analyzing the different ways in which money circulates and is used in the private and public spheres. In private firms, it is the pursuit of money that, in fact, "governs" organizational behaviour, while in the public sector, this role is taken, on the contrary, by the management of an already "acquired" money. For this reason, if one accepts the idea that money is a representative of the Symbolic and a semblance of the Other or, again, of the Father (according to the analytic and symbolic acceptation of the term: i.e., as bearer of reference and law), it appears that public services do not position the Father in the same place as do private firms (Guinchard, 1995)

In the case of the private sphere, one strives to "find" the Father (boss, director, rival, government, tax office) in order to pit oneself phallically against him, while, in the case of the public sphere, one is faced from the start with the presence of the "State", from which one demands a little bit extra each time, because this is precisely what it is there for (in order to underline that the 'nurturing mother' organization will always prove the stronger).

But the permanent omnipresence of the Father gives rise – as analytical case studies constantly remind us – to inhibition and a loss of the desire to act. Hence the all too understandable "hysteria" of all those public servants who do not feel sufficiently "recognized" and who stop work in order to make this known, fostering in this way a castration that is never symbolic enough. That being the case, the organizational consultant who is aware of the role of the signifier-seeming-money has good grounds for viewing certain decision-makers' attempts to apply management methods "just as they stand" from the private to the public sphere as a form of neurotic behaviour that aims at constructing a false-self. Or, to put it another way, we are faced here with a way of behaving that is based on a symbolic structure at odds with reality and that aims at attaining a goal without any risk of castration.

More generally, by meticulously observing the day to day reality of organizations, it becomes apparent that money, that seeming-Other, allows subjects – for reasons of psychical economy – to ignore the true Other that is the pivot of organizational action (Arnaud, 2002). It is a way, in sum, of avoiding any explicit questioning of the status of their desire and of the Father. Yet, in organizations as elsewhere, one should not give in to the illusions of the Symbolic-Seeming. Money and linguistic signifiers are unable to be the gauge of everything in the workplace – including subjects' "motivation", that avatar of desire that one never succeeds in "calibrating" or "translating" totally (in terms of either money or language). Moreover, as Lacan reminds us, Truth (with a capital "t") always remains inaccessible; one can at best, during an analysis, obtain certain truth-effects having therapeutic repercussions. By exploring and experimenting with the Symbolic – especially through the angle of money – what one comes to realize then is that it too, so to speak, has two sides: for one is led to take into account not only its strengths but also its weaknesses.

Notes

1. See: The Complete Letters of Sigmund Freud to Wilhelm Fliess 1887-1904, Cambridge, Massachusetts and London, England: The Belknap Press of Harvard University Press, 1985
2. This is true even in the case of gold. For gold is above all precious because it is money, and not the reverse, as Foucault (1971) reminds us.
3. Marx speaks, moreover, in Capital (1867), of a "universal equivalent in the world of merchandise".
4. This point concurs with Foucault's analyses of wealth as being, at once, an object of representation and of desire.
5. The face value of a bank note is a function of a standard measure, that is, the value or metal taken as references of the monetary system, according to a given convention.
6. Jean Baudrillard can therefore write:

   What makes money (gold) fascinating is neither its materiality nor the fact that it is the harnessed equivalent of a certain force (of labour) or virtual power, but, rather, its *systematicity* – the fact that this matter encloses the virtual total substitutability of all values due to their definitive abstraction. (1970, p. 217)

7. In 1990, Alain Minc published a book whose title, L'Argent Fou, is a play on words: in French "un argent fou" is a commonly used expression meaning "loads of money", but its literal sense is "mad money". [Translator's note.]

8. We are particularly thinking here of both the proverbial resistances of many elderly citizens – in France, for instance, there are senior citizens who still think today (some thirty years after the reevaluation of the franc) in terms of old francs – and the anxieties.

9. An emblematic illustration of these phenomena is given by Germany in 1923, when the currency depreciated at such a vertiginous rate at one stage that people very quickly found themselves having to spend thousands of millions of marks simply to ensure their everyday needs.

10. "*Jouissance*": there is no adequate translation in English of this word and most English translations of Lacan's texts retain the French. "*Jouissance*" shares a common etymology with the English word "enjoyment" (including the sense in which one can "enjoy rights and property"), but the latter has lost most of its former sexual connotations, while the French word simultaneously covers sexual, spiritual, and physical "enjoyment" or "ecstasy". [Translator's note]

References

Aglietta, M. & Orléan, A. (eds) (1998). *La monnaie souveraine*, Paris: Odile Jacob.

Arnaud, G. (1999). Quelques considération sur la fonction symbolique de l'argent pour la psychanalyse. *Revue internationale de psychosociologie*, 13: 37–49.

Arnaud, G. (2002). The organization and the symbolic: organizational dynamics viewed from a Lacanian perspective. *Human Relations*, 55 (4).

Arnaud, G. & Louart, P. (2000). Les gouvernances de l'argent: un point de vue psychanalytique. In: *Argent et gestion*, Toulouse: Presses Universitaires de Toulouse, pp. 321–329.

Assoun, P. L. et al. (1997.) *Psychanalyse*, Paris: Presses Universitaires de France.

Baudrillard, J. (1970). Fétichisme et idéologie: la réduction sémiologique. *Nouvelle revue de psychanalyse*, 2: 213–224.

Boltanski, L. & Thévenot, L. (1991). *De la justification*, Paris: Gallimard.

Borneman, E. (1978). *Psychanalyse de l'argent: Une recherche critique sur les théories psychanalytiques de l'argent*, Paris: Presses Universitaires de France.

Bouilloud, J-P. & Guienne, V. (eds) (1999). *Questions d'argent*, Paris: Desclée de Brouwer.

Chaskiel, P. (2000). L'étonnante neutralisation de la monnaie. *Sciences de la société*, 50–51.

Clerc, D. (2000). La monnaie: un vecteur du lien social. *Alternatives économiques*, 45(3): 25–27.

Collège de psychanalystes (1986). Série Psychanalystes, Volume 20, *Un patient est remboursé, Psychanalyse et argent*.

Collège de psychanalystes (1988). Série Psychanalystes, Volume 28, *L'argent, à nouveau*.

David, M. (1994). *Une psychanalyse amusante*, Paris: Epi-La Méridienne.

Droit, R-P. (ed.) (1992). *Comment penser l'argent?*, Paris: Le Monde.

Dufour, D-R. (1998). Serge Leclaire, l'invention d'une psychanalyse citoyenne. In: S. Leclaire (ed.), *Diableries. ecrits pour la psychanalyse 2*, Paris: Le Seuil/Arcanes, pp. 11–27.

Enriquez, E. (1997). *Les jeux du pouvoir et du désir dans l'entreprise*, Paris: Desclée de Brouwer.

Enriquez, E. (1999). L'argent, fétiche sacré. In J-P. Bouilloud and V. Guienne (eds), *Questions d'argent*, Paris: Desclée de Brouwer.

Fenichel, O. (1947). The drive to amass wealth. In: O. Fenichel and O. Rapoport (eds), *The Collected Papers of O. Fenichel*, New York: Norton.

Forman, N. (1987). *Mind over money*, Toronto: Doubleday.

Forrester, J. (1998). *Truth games: Lies, money and psychoanalysis*, Cambridge: Harvard University Press.

Foucault, M. (1971). *The order of things. An archaeology of the human sciences*, New York: Pantheon Books [originally published as: *Les mots et les choses. Une archéologie des sciences humaines*, Paris, Gallimard, 1966].

Freud, S. (1905). Three Essays on the Theory of Sexuality, SE7.

Freud, S. (1908). Character and anal erotism, SE9.

Freud, S. (1917). On transformations of instinct as exemplified in anal erotism, SE9.

Furnham, A. and Argyle, M. (1998). *The psychology of money*, London: Routledge.

Gardaz, M. (ed.) (1997). *Le surendettement des particuliers*, Paris: Anthropos.

Gide, A. (1931). *The counterfeiters* (trans. Dorothy Bussy), Harmondsworth, Middlesex: Penguin Books, 1966, p. 173 [originally published as: *Les faux-monnayeurs*, Paris: Gallimard, 1925].

Goldberg, H. & Lewis, R. (1978). *Money madness: The psychology of saving, Spending, loving and hating*, London: Springwood.

Gori, R. & Hoffmann, C. (1999). S'acquitter. In: *La science au risque de la psychanalyse*, Ramonville Saint-Agne: Erès, pp. 329–357.

Goux, J-J. (1984). *Les faux-monnayeurs du langage*, Paris: Editions Galilée.

Guillaume, M. (1992). Argent et hypermonnaie. In R-P. Droit (ed.), *Comment penser l'argent?*, Paris: Le Monde.

Guinchard, R. (1995). Père et fisc. In: *Une entreprise nommée désir*, Nice: IPM-CERAM.

Lacan, J. (1972). The seminar on The Purloined Letter (trans. J. Mehlman), *Yale French Studies*, 48: 39–72.

Le Mouël, J. (1991). *Critique de l'efficacité*, Paris: Le Seuil.

Martin, P. (1984). *Argent et psychanalyse*, Paris: Navarin.

Marx, K. (1867). *Capital*, Volume I (trans. E. and C. Paul), London: Dent, 1976.

Matthews, A. (1991). *If I think about money so much, why can't I figure it out?*, New York: Summit Books.

Minc, A. (1990). *L'Argent fou*, Paris: Grasset.

Reiss-Schimmel, I. (1993). *La psychanalyse et l'argent*, Paris: Odile Jacob.

Sagna, L. (2001). *Monnaie et sociétés. Une socio-anthropologie des pratiques monétaires*, Paris: L'Harmattan.

Schimmel, I. (1990). Vous êtes bien payée pour savoir ce que ça m'a coûté pour en arriver là. *Revue Française de Psychanalyse*, 54 (2): 533–552.

Simmel, G. (1900). *The philosophy of money* (trans. T. Bottomore and D. Frisby), London: Routledge, 1978.

Vallet, O. (1996). Les formes de pensée. In: A. de Mijolla and S. de Mijolla Mellor (eds), *Psychanalyse*, Paris: Presses Universitaires de France.

Viderman, S. (1992). *De l'argent en psychanalyse et au-delà*, Paris: Presses Universitaires de France.

INDEX